BREAK
FREE

from the cycle of
Destructive Relationships

BREAK
FREE

from the cycle of
Destructive Relationships

YOLANDA R. CUMBESS, JD

To Tierra Blessings to you and all you pursue!

Yolanda Cumb

purposely
created
PUBLISHING

**BREAK FREE FROM THE CYCLE OF
DESTRUCTIVE RELATIONSHIPS**

Published by Purposely Created Publishing Group™

Printed in the United States of America

ISBN: 978-1-949134-94-0

Special discounts are available on bulk quantity purchases by book clubs, associations and special interest groups. For details email: sales@publishyourgift.com or call (888) 949-6228.

For information log on to www.PublishYourGift.com

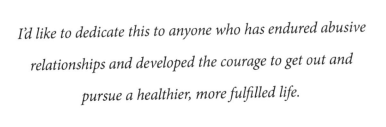

I'd like to dedicate this to anyone who has endured abusive relationships and developed the courage to get out and pursue a healthier, more fulfilled life.

TABLE OF CONTENTS

INTRODUCTION

I grew up in an unstable home in various parts of the inner city of Houston, Texas. My parents divorced when I was very young. We lived in poverty. My mother struggled with three kids as a single parent and we moved frequently. We were constantly changing schools and I moved several times between my mother and father, and sometimes my grandparents. Growing up, both my mother and my father were in a series of dysfunctional relationships and marriages. My mother has been married four different times with several boyfriends in between. None of my mother's marriages were healthy. My father has been married three different times. He also had live-in girlfriends. I witnessed my mother being physically beaten on multiple occasions by her second husband, and my mother, brother, and I were traumatized. He also physically attacked my brother and me, and we were terrified of him. On several occasions I called 911, risking my own safety because I feared for my mother's life. It was during this marriage that my sister was born. I never understood why my mom chose to stay, but I prayed for it to end. My brother and I wanted to run away from home. I learned to be passive in order to be safe, and to do what I was told. I never felt safe. Eventually my mother left him, and my sister never got to know her father.

My father's relationships were also destructive and marked with abuse. Although my father cared for me, he said many discouraging and hurtful things to my brother and me. I do not remember any of my parent's relationships being healthy, nor do I ever remember my parents being alone for long. My brother and I were separated due to the turmoil in my mother's home, and for his protection he moved to our father's home. My sister, who is 10 years younger than me, was a small child when I left for college.

I felt unloved as a child. It seemed my parents cared more about their relationships than the well-being of my brother and me. I know my parents love us, but they were incapable of showing us the validation, attention, and affection we needed. They were incapable of teaching me what was and was not acceptable in relationships, and neither were good role models. They were also incapable of showing my brother and me how we should allow others to treat us. As a result, I was bullied as a child and as a teenager. My view about what normal relationships looked like was completely dysfunctional. I now realize they did the best they could with what they knew, due to their own challenging experiences. But after witnessing my mother being abused, I vowed never to allow a man to hit me. I wanted to have a different life than my mother. I vowed to be successful, make the most of my education, and be independent.

Since I could not rely on my parents, I depended on myself. I pushed myself in school without much support from them. I set goals for myself and pursued them. I was determined to not let their indifference stop me. I was ambitious and academically successful, even landing an internship at the Johnson Space Center. I was a stand-out athlete, played junior Olympic volleyball, and eventually went to college on an athletic scholarship. Eventually, I obtained an engineering degree and a law degree, passed multiple bar exams, and obtained a job in my field where I advanced rather quickly.

Although I was successful in many areas of my life, my personal relationships were not so great. At the age of 17, I began to seek attention from men in all kinds of places. I soon started clubbing and my life was a revolving door of relationships with random men. I became pregnant during my senior year in high school by someone I did not know, and terminated the pregnancy to keep my scholarship to play collegiate volleyball. I was overly trusting and was repeatedly used, lied to, manipulated, and devalued. I dated all kinds, from highly paid, well-educated men, to average working men and unstable men. While in college I became infatuated with a very intelligent man who was in law school. I was obsessed with him. Our relationship was lopsided and he was very possessive and manipulative. However, I admired him and did not understand how I should be treated in a relationship. After being involved with him for three years, he impregnated me at the age of 22, after which he wanted nothing to do with me. I reluctantly agreed to terminate the pregnancy, but I was deeply hurt. Soon after, he came back and I saw him again. I eventually found the courage to leave the relationship and went to law school.

For the next few years, I entertained numerous disappointing, dead-end relationships. I was not interested in love, only companionship and support. I did not know what love felt like. At 27, after graduating from law school, I began dating an assistant district attorney and was sexually assaulted by him. I couldn't believe what happened to me and I was afraid to speak up for fear that no one would believe me. Early in the relationship he lost his temper with me for not doing something he wanted, however I did not know that this was a sign of abuse. After each outburst he apologized and I forgave him. I became passive and I knew he was not faithful, but I didn't say anything. One morning, I found myself running from his house after a violent outburst and had to get dressed in a Waffle House restroom before work. Eventually, I accepted that I was in a violent relationship, and that I was in danger. When I left, he began calling me nonstop from an unknown number. I called the police but was told that they could not help me. I cut off all contact, and a few months later, I moved to DC to accept my position with the Patent Office. A year later someone reached out to me to inform me that he had assaulted another lady. I supported her and encouraged her to press charges. I vowed to never again be silent when I experience abuse.

My first serious relationship was at age 30, and I was seriously deceived. He was a few years older than me. He was tall, attractive, and well-educated. He was also a retired high-ranking Army officer. He made many false promises of marriage and was very demanding of my time and attention. I ended the relationship when I realized he was lying and stringing me along. I became depressed and at 31 I was diagnosed as an alcoholic. I was warned by mental health professionals that if I did not get treatment I would destroy my life or die. I declined rehabilitation and moved back to Atlanta for a fresh start.

Soon after moving to Atlanta, at age 32, I impulsively married a man after three months of dating because I was tired of being constantly hurt and disappointed. I thought this was a logical way out. He was recently divorced and was down on his luck. But, I had compassion for him. I knew he wasn't perfect, but he was charming and seemed really nice. He told me he loved me and promised me his loyalty, forever. He was well-liked by many people and he even joined my church. Although he didn't have much to offer materially, I was lonely and wanted a family. I wanted out of the constant turmoil in my life. So, I gave him a chance while helping him get on his feet. He had a son with his previous spouse, and he told me that he might have a baby on the way with another woman, but I married him anyway. He said that he was unsure if he had fathered the child and persuaded me that the other woman was trying to take advantage of him. As a matter of fact, every woman from his past was manipulative, crazy, dishonest, and selfish. He was always the victim. I believed his stories. I wanted to prove to him that I was different.

The marriage to him became the most emotionally abusive and destructive relationship I have ever experienced, and in less than two years, it had wreaked complete havoc in my life. He moved in with me and I was the main financial supporter. I frequently took time off work to assist him with legal matters pertaining to his children. I took on every problem in his life as if it were my own, even caring for both of his children. I was deeply affectionate and loyal and did everything I could do to honor my husband. My entire existence revolved around him and his children. But somehow my efforts were never good enough.

Within a few months of being married, his behavior became increasingly erratic and unpredictable. One moment he was Dr. Jekyl and the next he was Mr. Hyde. I was frequently yelled at and criticized without warning or rational explanation. Many times I was ignored or punished for doing exactly what he asked. He started arguments and no matter how I responded, I was to blame.

He was also extremely possessive and constantly questioned my loyalty. I thought this was a sign of love. At his request, I cut contact with friends and I made sure he knew where I was at all times. I felt imprisoned, and I was deeply committed to him. But the more I did for him, the less he respected me. When I tried to explain what was going on to other members of the marriage ministry at church, I was seen as the villain. When I confided in my family, no one believed me.

I hated our conflicts, so I always gave in to keep the peace. Despite the constant turmoil, he still managed to convince me that he loved me. I had compassion for him, since I was in a more stable place than him.

I had gone into my marriage financially stable. I had a few friends and was successful in my career. But by the end, I was so severely mentally fatigued and depressed that I could hardly function. I was so stressed from enduring nonstop emotional abuse and helping my husband with all of his issues, that I had neglected myself. My work performance plummeted and my career was in jeopardy. My life was crumbling to the point of no repair. To save my career, I moved back to DC. I knew things were going incredibly wrong.

My husband tricked me into thinking that he would join me when he found employment. But within three of weeks of my separation, I found out that he was having multiple, simultaneous affairs with dozens of women unbeknownst to me. My husband was a con artist and I was being betrayed. My husband had been deliberately lying to me and manipulating me from the very beginning. I was in complete shock. When I confronted him, he acted with complete indifference towards me. I filed for divorce and we parted ways. I never looked back, but I was devastated by his level of deception and lack of empathy. Although my marriage lasted less than two years, it took many more years to rebuild my life and my mental health after my divorce.

Just prior to finalizing my divorce, I met an even more attractive, charming man. He was a Navy veteran, educated, and was much more financially stable. He too had promised me the future and swept me off of my feet. I knew we were moving fast, but I didn't care. He showered me with gifts and attention. I got pregnant and although it wasn't ideal, I was happy because I wanted a child. As it turned out, his behavior was even scarier than my ex-husband's. My new man, and the father of my unborn child, had an explosive temper and he showed early signs of being both physically and emotionally abusive. This time, it wasn't easy to just walk away, so we decided to try to work things out.

Almost halfway into the pregnancy, I unexpectedly suffered a traumatic miscarriage that nearly took my life. I had gone to the doctor's office after experiencing unusual symptoms, but they assured me that nothing was wrong and sent me home, not realizing that the baby was in danger and I was in labor. The next morning I went to the emergency room. I experienced major complications and was fighting for my life. I was hospitalized for two days, alone. I left in a taxi cab since I had no one to take me home. I told the nurses I had no other choice. I was devastated beyond any level I had ever experienced before. I had no baby, no support, and it seemed like my life was in shambles. I was experiencing major postpartum depression, but I had nothing to show for it.

I ended the relationship with my child's father since I knew it was not healthy. I did not have any close connections and no one really understood the severity of my experiences. I was on the verge of a complete nervous breakdown. I had finally reached my breaking point and I reached out to God because I had no one else to turn to. I knew that if my life didn't change, I was going to die. I was so angry. I didn't understand why my life was in such turmoil. I was a good person, yet despite my kindness, no one was there for me when I needed them the most.

I wanted to understand why all these men who seemed so great, treated me so poorly. It was mind-boggling how I kept finding myself in the same situation, over and over. I didn't understand why I had no friends to count on when I was so reliable. So, I asked God for revelation and started studying the nature of abusive relationships. Initially, I didn't consider my previous relationships to be abusive. I didn't understand the severity of the abuse I had endured, or the danger I was putting myself in.

As I meditated and studied God's Word, I began to understand how much God loved me and that it was not His desire for me to be committed to people who were harming me. I learned that there should be healthy limits on my interactions with others. I gained a better understanding of how we are to relate to each other and what godly relationships look like. I also learned the value of doing things God's way, which protects us from unnecessary heartache and grief. By being open to change, following God's Word, and embracing my identity in Christ, God gave me the grace to break away from the chains of destructive relationships, and to boldly pursue the life that He had for me. I am now walking in my purpose.

It seems unnatural to think that relationships can be dangerous to your well-being. I knew that physical abuse in relationships was wrong, but I did not know that abuse does not have to be physical to be harmful. However, I discovered that even when relationships are not physically harmful, other types of abuse can have an equally destructive impact on your life.

It is my goal to help you make better relationship choices so that you don't find yourself giving your love away to those who don't deserve it, constantly having to pick up the pieces in your life. It is also my desire to help you achieve victory in your life by letting go of past hurt, forgiving others, and embracing your identity in Christ so that you can walk in your purpose.

CHAPTER 1
WHAT IS A DESTRUCTIVE RELATIONSHIP?

Scriptures

Proverbs 4:23 KJV: "Keep thy heart with all diligence, for out of it are the issues of life."

1 Peter 5:8 KJV: "Be sober, be vigilant; because your adversary the devil, as a roaring lion, walketh about, seeking whom he may devour:"

Matthew 7:15 KJV: "Beware of the false prophets, which come to you in sheep's clothing, but inwardly they are ravening wolves."

Overcome Destructive Relationships

After spending many years going from one destructive relationship to the next, it was clear that I did not know what a healthy relationship looked like. But in subsequent years, through prayer and studying various material on abusive relationships and God's Word, I learned that there are certain patterns of behavior for individuals who are dysfunctional and abusive. I also learned about people who possess godly traits and are healthy. My goal is to help you identify destructive traits in yourself and others so that you do not needlessly suffer or waste time in relationships that are harmful to you. This book gives insight and serves as an introduction to recognizing and overcoming harmful relationships by obeying God's Word, walking in your purpose, and knowing your identity in Christ.

The information presented should not be relied upon solely. It is critical that you do your own research and self-reflection regarding abusive relationships and developing a healthy approach to relationships. While this book is targeted to help women overcome abuse, men can apply the same principles as well. Additionally, the concepts presented are not limited to romantic relationships but can apply to relationships with family members and friends.

Identify Destructive People

The first step to avoiding a destructive relationship is to be able to identify signs of a potentially harmful partner before the relationship begins. For most of us, if we knew a person was harmful we would not choose to become involved with them. But, in many instances, a person who is abusive appears to be a wonderful person. Often, abusers are too good to be true. They are often highly-respected, attractive, and accomplished. Some abusers profess to be devout Christians, holding high positions in church. Nevertheless, a highly-respected, Bible quoting, and seemingly "good" man can hurt you.

What determines how a man will treat you is his character. It is possible to have respectable qualities and do good things while having very poor character. Matthew 7:15 KJV says to "Beware of the false prophets, which come to you in sheep's clothing, but inwardly they are ravening wolves." No one expects a sheep to be a wolf. Your goal is to discern the difference between the two. To identify a destructive person, you must be on full alert. Pay close attention to the words and actions of a man you are admiring and trust your gut instinct. Don't be easily enticed by attention, flattery, and gifts. Someone coming on very strong when you meet him is often covering up major character flaws. This is the first major indicator of an unhealthy person. By noticing key behavior patterns and learning to ask the right questions, you can better perceive a person's character and intentions. Be careful of what you share if you are in a vulnerable place emotionally. Predators often use what you share to make you think that they care and to then take advantage of you. Predators know that you can easily be enticed when you are vulnerable.

Types of Abusers

ANTISOCIAL PERSONALITY DISORDER

In order to get a better understanding of how abusive relationships begin, it is helpful to know some of the traits of abusive individuals. Abusers often exhibit traits of someone with an antisocial personality disorder. A person with this disorder has "a pervasive pattern of disregard for and violation of the rights of others," as indicated by at least three of the following:

1. "Failure to conform to social norms with respect to lawful behaviors."

2. "Deceitfulness," "use of aliases," or "conning others for personal profit or pleasure."

3. "Impulsivity or failure to plan ahead."

4. "Irritability and aggressiveness," repeatedly involved in "physical fights or assaults."

5. "Reckless disregard for safety of self or others."

6. "Consistent irresponsibility," including a repeated failure to maintain employment or "honor financial obligations."

7. "Lack of remorse," indicated by "being indifferent to" or rationalizing hurting, mistreatment, or stealing from another.[12]

1. Sociopath

A sociopath is someone with a mental condition "who consistently shows no regard for right and wrong and ignores the rights and feelings of others"[13] A sociopath is defined as someone having an antisocial personality disorder, "which is characterized by a long-standing pattern of disregarding other people's rights."[12] Sociopaths manipulate and treat others harshly or with callous indifference to get their needs met. A sociopath has a very weak conscience and shows little remorse for their behavior.[14, 15] Sociopaths are often pathological liars and may "behave violently or impulsively." They may also "have problems with drugs or alcohol."[13]

2. Psychopath

A psychopath is a type of sociopath who is completely incapable of feeling guilt, remorse, or empathy.[14, 15] A true psychopath "does not have a conscious," making them especially dangerous.[15] Psychopaths have shallow feelings, and know the difference between right and wrong, but dismiss rules as if they don't apply to them. Psychopaths are hard to spot because they are manipulating and cunning and can blend seamlessly into society.[14, 15, 16, 17]

3. Narcissistic Personality Disorder

Narcissistic personality disorder is another type of antisocial personality disorder. Narcissistic personality disorder is a mental condition in which a person "has an inflated sense of his own importance, as well as a deep need for excessive attention and admiration."[18] Behind a narcissistic person's "extreme confidence lies a fragile self-esteem that is vulnerable to the slightest criticism."[18] From a biblical perspective, someone having this disorder has an issue with pride. Pride is a sin and God hates pride (Proverbs 8:13).

Philippians 2:4, NIV says, "not looking to your own interests but each of you to the interests of the others." Because of their lack of empathy a person with a narcissistic personality disorder tends to have difficult relationships.[18] Narcissistic people tend to be drawn towards empaths and codependents, people who show tremendous care for the feelings of others. Codependents are attractive to a narcissistic person due to their willingness to deny their own needs to cater to another's desires.

4. Other Toxic Personality Types

a. The User

This type of man excessively relies on others to take care of him. He does not mind taking advantage of the kindness of others. He is the type of man that expects you to take care of him and possibly his children. He is irresponsible and extremely entitled. He likes to have nice things, yet he lacks the discipline or motivation to earn the things he desires. He is unreliable and is not available when you need something. This type of man claims he cannot afford child support, yet he entertains women. This type of abuser shows no accountability for his choices but blames others for his problems.

b. The Victim

Related to The User is a man I call, The Victim. The Victim displays traits of someone who is codependent. Codependent relationships are dysfunctional relationships "where one person relies on the other person to meet nearly all of their emotional needs," while [the other person enables their partner to maintain this irresponsible, addictive, or underachieving behavior].[19] In codependent relationships, "two people become so invested in each other that they can't function independently anymore."[19] "One person's mood, happiness, and identity" is wrapped up in the other person.[20]

When you meet The Victim, he is in distress. Drama surrounds his life and the problem is never him. The rescuer (nurturer) inside of you desperately wants to help him so much that you are willing to neglect your own needs. After all, he's a good man deep down, and you know that if you help him, he will be eternally grateful for you. He lost his job, so you write his resume, buy him clothes for his interview, and clean up his image. He promises to return the favor when he gets on his feet. Soon you begin managing his life. He just needs some uplifting. Now you're doing all the work, and eventually you begin to resent him. Instead of feeling appreciated, you realize that you're being used and completely taken for granted.

c. The Rich Guy

The Rich Guy is wealthy and successful. He does not expect you to take care of him like The User, but your relationship is devoid of real affection and love. He worked very hard to get to where he is, overcoming extraordinary circumstances. He has a fancy home, nice things, and a lot of clout. He is attractive and women wish to be in your shoes. Everything is about his business ventures, his ideas, and his problems. You take a back seat to everything he does. You are an accessory to him. You fear that if you leave him he will quickly replace you. Because The Rich Guy has no time for you, he buys you things and gives you money. You think you should be happy to be with The Rich Guy, but you are not. People think you are the ideal couple. They don't know how empty your relationship is, nor do they know how lonely you feel. You are ignored while he travels to do important things with important people. When you are together, you are ignored and people see you as a trophy. This relationship feels more like a business arrangement. It is tempting to settle for The Rich Guy after you've been hurt. However, without mutual love you will not be happy with him since real love cannot be purchased.

4. Mr. Self-Centered

Self-centered people are harmful because they require excessive attention and admiration to the demise of the other person. Just like the narcissistic person, a relationship with a self-centered person is lopsided since you do all the giving, and he shows no real interest in your needs. This man requests that you put your career goals on hold, while he pursues his own professional endeavors. After you have invested years in the relationship, he leaves you for another person. Selfish people expect you to take off from work and be available for them at the drop of a dime. He becomes agitated when you try to confront his selfish ways. A selfish person ignores your boundaries, and treats your time, money, and affection as if they own them. Selfish people can be possessive, since they are constantly threatened by the real possibility that you will wake up and leave them. It's not because he loves you. Your leaving takes away a source for having his needs met.

e. The Addict

People who abuse alcohol or drugs are not safe persons to be romantically involved with. According to an article titled "How Drug Abuse Hurts Relationships" on drugabuse.com, drug addicts are primarily controlled by their addiction. People who are addicted to drugs are solely focused on obtaining the substance. [21] Drug abusers "will lie about where they were, who they were with, or where the money went" out of guilt. Drug addicts can be secretive, isolated, and are emotionally unstable due to the drugs. [21] Drugs are known to increase anger, irritability, and violence, making an addict potentially dangerous. Even a functional alcoholic may engage in impulsive behavior and poor choices that put you or him in harm's way. Drug addicts are also financially unstable since they spend all their money, or yours, on drugs. [21]

f. The Criminal

A criminal is also someone you should stay away from. Involvement with this type of person exposes you to danger due to their lack of regard for social rules. [22] Criminals are much more likely to resort to violent behavior to get their needs met. A person with a history of being violent towards others can be violent towards you. The criminal can also get you caught up in his illegal activity by asking you to do unlawful things for him, putting you at risk for going to prison.[22] It is hard to maintain a relationship with someone who is in and out of jail. It is even harder for children with absent parents because one or both are incarcerated.

A person with a criminal past must go through significant rehabilitation and demonstrate that he is completely reformed.

g. The Inconsistent Guy

Mr. Inconsistent is hot and cold. One day he adores you and the next day you wonder if he really cares, probably because he is entertaining multiple women. You're not really in a real relationship, yet you care for him deeply. Your involvement with him is an emotional roller coaster. He future-baits, then changes his mind. His behavior is inconsistent, making you question if he really means what he says. He disappears for days or weeks and then mysteriously reappears as if nothing ever happened. He doesn't offer any explanation for his disappearance, yet somehow you stay in contact. He claims he's not ready for a commitment yet, but he knows just what to say and do to keep you holding on.

h. The Player

Although infidelity was discussed above, The Player needs to be mentioned. This man has a reputation for the ladies that is well-deserved. He likes all the flavors, and women tolerate him, including you. The Player knows exactly what to say and do to get your attention, despite indications that he is entertaining other women. You're not really in a relationship with The Player, but he seems very into you and you hope that he'll change for you. However, The Player is not into you, he is into his ego. He does not love you or anyone else. He is not thinking about the future consequences of his philandering ways. Healthy relationships are based on trust. Without trust, you cannot feel safe. If he claims to commit to you, you will be suspicious and insecure. You cannot earn a person's commitment. A man does not suddenly become loyal to you because you are better than the rest. A man is loyal because he is mature and responsible, and he genuinely cares about the feelings of others. Someone claiming to love you while remaining disloyal is not someone you should entertain.

What is Relationship Abuse?

"Abuse is a pattern of behaviors one person uses to gain and maintain power and control over their partner."[1] There are many types of abusive relationships, and not all abuse is physical. Relationship abuse may also be sexual or emotional. Relationship abuse may occur in friendships and within families. All abusive relationships are harmful and no form of abuse is okay.

Avoiding or ending abusive relationships is important since these relationships have far-reaching effects on many aspects of your life as well as the lives of others. Not only do abusive relationships affect you, but they may also endanger your children, other family members, and anyone you may be remotely connected to. Moreover, toxic relationships prevent you from becoming your best self and living the life that God desires for you.

Shooting at First Baptist Church of Sutherland Springs

On November 5, 2017, Devin Patrick Kelley shot and killed 26 people and wounded 20 others at First Baptist Church in Sutherland Springs, Texas. Even though Kelley had a history of domestic violence during his previous marriage and was also arrested for various assault charges, he managed to marry again. Before the shooting, it appears that Kelley was sending threatening text messages to his mother-in-law, who attended the church.[2]

This is one of many notorious examples of how abuse in a romantic relationship can escalate to the point where innocent people are harmed. More than likely, Kelley's wife never suspected that her husband was capable of such an evil act, despite his clear history of abuse. While Kelley's wife is not to blame for the horrendous actions of her husband, she might not have made the choice to be involved with him if she recognized early how dangerous he was. There are many other stories in the news just like hers, where abuse in the relationship led to the horrendous loss of lives—that of the partner and other innocent people.

Far-Reaching Effects of Abuse

Abuse takes a serious emotional and even financial toll on victims and it can take years for them to recover. Many women die each year. According to a CDC report published in 2017, the majority of the murders of women were committed by a current or former romantic partner.[3] But abused partners are not the only ones who suffer in abusive relationships. Children are also adversely impacted. It is not possible for you to allow yourself to be abused and still provide the protection, love, and support your children need to develop into healthy, secure, well-adjusted adults. Abusive relationships suffocate you, distort your priorities, and make you less available to devote time and attention to your children and yourself. Moreover, a person who abuses you can abuse your children too. Children cannot adequately protect themselves from an abuser, so it is your responsibility to protect your children from being abused or witnessing abuse. Unfortunately, there are many instances where a romantic partner or spouse sexually assaults, physically abuses, or murders the child of the other partner.

Children are deeply influenced by their parent's behavior and parents are the most significant role models for children. Children also tend to normalize abuse when they are exposed to it and often repeat the same cycles of destructive behavior. Men who were exposed to domestic violence as children are three to four times more likely to become violent partners than men who were not.[4] Women also repeat patterns of tolerating abuse they witnessed when seeing their mother being abused. This perpetuates generational cycles of the same behavior.

Therefore, for your own interests and the interests of your loved ones, it is critical that you approach your relationships cautiously. Proverbs 4:23 KJV says to "Keep thy heart with all diligence, for out of it are the issues of life." Abuse lowers your self-esteem, distorts your true identity, and limits your personal growth. Consequently, you become more susceptible to future destructive relationships.

Because of the far-reaching impact of abuse, it is important to carefully consider anyone you are thinking about dating. It is critical to get to know a person's character over a significant period of time before you become emotionally attached, since it is easier to identify the negative traits a person possesses when you are just getting to know them. If you become emotionally attached too soon, you miss things that you otherwise would have questioned.

Red Flags

In auto racing, a flagman waves a red flag to signal when conditions are too hazardous for a driver to continue. When the red flag is waved, the driver must stop, or he or she may be hurt.[5] In relationships, red flags are indicators that the person is hazardous to you and signals major problems in the future.[6] Abusive individuals display red flags. If you are alert, you can discern inconsistencies in moral character, even when they are subtle. The apostle Peter instructs us to "Be sober, be vigilant; because your adversary the devil, as a roaring lion, walketh about, seeking whom he may devour" 1 Peter 5:8 KJV. When you see a red flag, you should stop and further evaluate the person's character before proceeding. Depending on the circumstances, you may even need to stop communication altogether.

Red Flags of Abuse

Listed below are some typical red flags, which indicate that a person is abusive. This information is taken from the NNEDV (National Network to End Domestic Violence).[7] Common red flags of an abuser is someone who:

- Has abused other people.

- Wants to rush into a relationship.

- Excessively showers you with attention early in the relationship.

- Is possessive and controlling and wants you to stop spending time with others, or wants you to stop all other activities.

- Is excessively jealous. Contacts you frequently throughout the day.

- Does not respect your boundaries.

- Makes you feel unworthy. Calls you names, or puts you down.

- Purposely ignores you when he can't get what he wants.

- Never accepts responsibility for his choices and instead blames others. Blames the demise of all his relationships on his former partners.

- Takes your money or possessions, or wants to control your finances. Has an uncontrollable temper.

- Is violent towards you, or has threatened to harm or kill you or others.
- Threatens to commit suicide.

Physical Abuse

Physical abuse, is a well-known and more obvious type of abuse. Physical abuse occurs when a partner uses violence to injure his victim to control or intimidate or "otherwise hurt her."[8]

The goal of a physical abuser is to intimidate his victims to have control over them. Physical abuse is not based on love, but it is a display of power by the abuser to boost his ego. Victims of physical abuse learn to become passive to avoid an attack. Violence typically escalates as the relationship progresses, and the violent behavior by the abuser is cyclical. The abuser has a violent outburst, then apologizes. The abuser eventually has another violent outburst, and the cycle repeats itself.[8]

Examples of Physical Abuse

- A man threatens to kill his wife if she leaves him.
- A man pushes his girlfriend.
- A man kicks his pregnant girlfriend in the stomach.

Sexual Abuse

Sexual abuse "refers to sexual contact or behavior that occurs without explicit consent of the victim."[9] Most sexual abuse victims know their abusers. Sexual abuse in a relationship can occur along with physical and emotional abuse.[9] Sexual abuse is not limited to unmarried couples and may happen between a husband and a wife. Children can also be sexually abused. This type of abuse deeply impacts a victim emotionally and psychologically.[10]

Examples of Sexual Abuse

- A boyfriend forcing sex on his partner while on a date.
- A husband forces his children to watch him have sex with their mother.
- A man has sex with a woman when she is incapacitated.

Emotional (Psychological) Abuse

Emotional abuse, also referred to as psychological abuse, is a harmful, subtler form of abuse. An emotional or psychological abuser adversely tries to control you by negatively affecting your thoughts and feelings.[11] Emotional abuse occurs when someone insults, yells, threatens, mocks, ignores, or rejects you to "intimidate, degrade, and control" you.[11] Emotional abusers lie, accuse, humiliate, or use any other cruel behavior to diminish how you feel about yourself.

Emotional abusers can be hard to spot since they tend to be very charming. Psychological abusers are masters of manipulation. Their popularity and appeal to others can discourage a victim from speaking out. They are good at convincing you and others that you are the problem, or getting you to question your memory of events, when clearly the abuser's behavior is to blame. Emotional abusers use blame-shifting tactics to make you feel guilty for their mistreatment towards you. These types of abusers are so good at manipulating you, you may not realize that you are being taken advantage of. Emotionally abusive relationships ultimately have you walking on eggshells to avoid conflict.

Examples of Emotional Abuse

- Your partner uses crazy-making behavior, referred to as gaslighting. For example, your partner says his favorite meal is Mexican and you make tacos. When you make it, he asks, "Why did you cook this?" You explain that he told you he liked Mexican. Then he says, "I never said that. I hate Mexican, I like Chinese."

- Your partner says something mean, laughs, and then says, "I'm just kidding."

- Your partner humiliates you in front of others.

Liars, Cheaters, and Philanderers

Another form of an emotionally destructive relationship is a relationship with a pathological liar or cheater. Lying and cheating demonstrates a selfish disregard for your feelings and your safety. Cheating is never excusable and you cannot cause someone to cheat. Cheating creates lopsided relationships, with the cheater demanding your loyalty and respect without giving you the same loyalty or respect in return. In addition to generating deep feelings of rejection in you, your involvement with an unfaithful person potentially exposes you to danger, like a sexually transmitted disease, or a violent confrontation from another lover. How many stories have you read involving romantic partners who were murdered because of an affair or a jealous ex? Cheating behavior also presents the risks of conceiving a child by another romantic partner.

Whether the abuse is physical, sexual, or emotional, you should not tolerate mistreatment in a relationship. You should not stay in an abusive relationship based on an abuser's promises to change. Many abusers do not believe they have a problem and therefore do not have the capacity to change. An abuser must demonstrate a sincere willingness to change in addition to receiving extensive spiritual and psychological guidance. Your love cannot save him.

Prayer:
Dear Heavenly Father, help me to distinguish between destructive relationships and healthy ones. Reveal to me harmful behavior patterns in others and give me the wisdom to respond appropriately. Amen.

Healthy Conflict
In a healthy relationship two people can disagree and respect each other's opinions without judgment or ridicule.

Healthy conflict does not require yelling, intimidation, or name-calling. It is impossible to always agree with another person. However, in a healthy relationship, you are allowed to have an opinion. In loving relationships, each person is equally respected. If you find yourself walking on eggshells for fear that your partner is going to respond negatively, it is your sign to exit the relationship immediately. Abusive relationships do not get better over time, they get worse.

The bottom line when dealing with a person who possesses destructive characteristics is that the relationship is not based on love. An abuser does not have the capacity to truly love you because of his own serious mental and emotional issues. Although he can be nice at times, his kindness is not consistent or sincere. Instead, it is often a ploy to manipulate you into staying in the relationship or getting what he wants. Get out once you identify someone possessing these toxic traits. If you believe that you are in danger, please contact the following resources for help: The National Domestic Violence Hotline: 1-800-799-SAFE (7233) or TTY 1-800-787-3224; hotline.womenslaw.org.[23]

Prayer:
Dear Heavenly Father, please give me the wisdom to be able to recognize harmful behavior in others quickly. Help me to become more aware of who I'm letting get close to me. Give me the wisdom to ask the right questions and the strength to leave when necessary. Amen.

CHAPTER 2
AUTHENTIC LOVE

Scripture

1 Corinthians 13:4-7 NIV: "Love is patient, love is kind. It does not envy, it does not boast, it is not proud. It does not dishonor others, it is not self-seeking, it is not easily angered, it keeps no record of wrongs. Love does not delight in evil but rejoices with the truth. It always protects, always trusts, always hopes, always perseveres."

Authentic Love is Godly Love

The Bible teaches us that authentic love is kind and is not self-seeking. In Mark 12:30-31 NIV, God commands us to love our neighbors as we love ourselves. Love is the fulfillment of God's law, as we are told in Romans 13:10 NIV. Any person who abuses you physically, emotionally, or sexually is acting out of pride and selfishness, not love. Abuse is the opposite of love. To understand love is to understand God's character. No love can compare to God's love for you. God is love (1 John 4:8).

God loves you and desires to bless you. The Bible says that Christ came so that we may have life and have life more abundantly. It is not God's desire for us to suffer in an abusive relationship. God does not desire for you to live in fear in a relationship or constantly worry that your spouse is cheating. Why would Christ suffer and die for you, for you to endure abuse by a man?

Love is Sacrificial

Real love is sacrificial. Christ's love for us is so great that He took on the sins of the world and died for all of mankind. Christ did no wrong. He died for people who rejected Him. You did not do anything to deserve Christ's love and you cannot do anything to make Him stop loving you.

A man who truly loves you will make sacrifices for you. To sacrifice means to give up something very important for a greater good. Love is not based on convenience. Although a man can never love you the way that God loves you, he'll gladly forfeit many things to show you he loves you. A man who loves you will risk his life for you. He'll give you whatever he has. He will go out of his way. He'll go hungry; he'll work overtime; he'll work jobs he does not like to provide. He willingly does things he may not want to do, just to see you happy. A man who loves you makes sacrifices because pleasing you is more important than his desires! He'll make sacrifices without resentment or expecting you to make the same sacrifices as him. It is God's desire for you to experience love that is sacrificial, like His.

Love is Consistent

God is faithful and His love is consistent and never failing. God's love is reliable and He'll never leave you or forsake you. He loved you before you were born and His affection for you is infinite. God's love for you does not change based on circumstances, what you did, or even how you treat

Him. The Bible teaches us that God's mercies are new every morning (Lamentations 3:23).

Malachi 3:6 NIV and Hebrews 13:8 NIV tells us that God does not change and Jesus is the same yesterday, today, and forever more. Even when we abandon God, He never abandons us. You will never have to wonder if He will be there. Take a moment to reflect on how faithful God has been to you.

True love does not change from one moment to the next. Love is not confusing or unreliable. When a man loves you, you know it. He wants you to be sure about his love. He clearly expresses his love for you and his love is not fleeting. A man who loves you will not love you today and reject you tomorrow. He is faithful and dependable; he understands that he can't love you and someone else at the same time. A person who can't make up his mind about you does not love you. Confusion is not a characteristic of love, but signifies lust. Also, because love is consistent, true love takes time to develop. "Love" that develops quickly is probably lust, which is based on selfish impulses and only seeks to please the flesh. Lust is destructive.

Love is Kind

True love is kind and is not easily angered. God is kind. God's kindness is unfailing; He loves us with an everlasting love (Jeremiah 31:3). His lovingkindness is better than life (Psalm 63:3). God is gracious and compassionate, and He wants to bless you simply because He loves you. His grace is a gift. God did not save us based on our deeds, but because

He loves us and wants to have an intimate relationship with us. It is only because of His grace that we can inherit His kingdom through His son Jesus. God is not easily angered, but He is merciful. The Bible says His mercy endures forever (Psalm 118:2). God does not cut us off when we mess up, but He is quick to forgive. God hates sin because sin is destructive. Even though we deserve to die because of our sins, God decided to let those who believe in His son, Jesus, live an abundant life on Earth.

A man who loves you is kind. He shows compassion and gentleness towards you. A loving man is understanding. He wants to know what makes you happy and what makes you unhappy. He sincerely cares about your needs and he likes to please you. He will not want to hurt or intentionally do unkind things to cause you pain. He will not play games, hit you, or put you down. A loving man will not easily lose his temper or display anger. All people make mistakes, but someone who loves you rarely mistreats you. He will not consistently or intentionally make you feel bad.

Love Protects

Authentic love wants to protect you. God is our protector. He is our "refuge" and "our shield" (2 Samuel 22:3). He is our stronghold. He fights for us and He saves us from our enemies (2 Samuel 22:3 NIV). There is no one mightier than God. The Bible says God is "a strong tower: the righteous runneth into it, and is safe" (Proverbs 18:10 KJV).

When the children of Israel were in Egypt, God shielded them from the plagues that killed the Egyptians. When the children of Israel were fleeing from the grips of their oppressors, God parted the waters of the Red Sea to allow the children of Israel to cross. Pharaoh and his army were swallowed up. Psalm 23:1 KJV declares that the Lord is our shepherd. A shepherd is responsible for his flock and provides for all the various needs of the sheep. He feeds his flock and protects his sheep from being eaten by wolves, taken by thieves, and going astray. Similarly, God provides for us and protects us from dangers seen and unseen. He leads us when we go astray. God fights for you when you have no one. God is a "father to the fatherless, a defender of widows" (Psalm 68:5 NIV). Think about how God has protected you.

A man who loves you wants to protect you. He wants to shield you from hurt and harm, and he will protect you with his life. Like a good shepherd, he wants to provide for your needs, not leave you wandering around aimlessly or wondering where your next meal is coming from. A man who loves you wants you to feel safe. The Bible says, "There is no fear in love. But perfect love drives out fear" (1 John 4:18 NIV). True love does not expose you to harm by putting you in dangerous situations, depriving you, intimidating you, or making you feel insecure. A loving man will never neglect you or leave you fending for yourself. Love builds up, it does not tear down.

Love is Patient

God's love is patient. God eagerly waits for us. He does not pressure us into a relationship with Him, but always welcomes us with open arms. God meets us where we are and walks with us even when we don't acknowledge Him and even when we aren't aware He is there. God's love does not condemn or scorn, but He gently corrects us when we are wrong. God does not wipe us off the earth when we are disobedient. Numbers 14:18 ESV declares, "The Lord is slow to anger and abounding in steadfast love, forgiving iniquity and transgression." When the children of Israel complained and chose to not obey the Lord's commandments in the wilderness, God remained with them. Acts 13:18 proclaims that for forty years He put up with them in the wilderness. He never gave up on them. God's love never gives up on you.

Similarly, a man who loves you is patient. He will not pressure you into a relationship, a marriage, sex, or anything else. A loving man does not mind waiting. He wants you to be comfortable with him. He is considerate and will not place unreasonable demands on you. A loving man does not expect you to suddenly drop everything for him. A man who cares for you understands that your time and energy are valuable. He will not become angry when he is disappointed. He will not walk away from you for not giving him what he wants. He hopes for you and knows that you are worth waiting for.

Love Respects

The epitome of love is respect. Love cannot exist without respect. To respect means to hold in high regard, to high esteem; to appreciate or to admire.[24] God cherishes you and holds you in high regard. You are the center of his affection. You are God's masterpiece, his workmanship (Ephesians 2:10 KJV). He is constantly thinking of you (Psalm 139:17-18 KJV). He adores you and is thinking of you right now. God's admiration for us is so deep that when man fell out of relationship with Him because of man's disobedience, He sent His son to die for us so that we could live (1 John 4:9).

A man who loves you respects you. He admires you and holds you in high esteem. He is proud of you and is honored to be with you. He does not want to change you but gladly accepts you as you are. He appreciates you. He celebrates your accomplishments and is not envious when you are successful. He views your success as an asset, not a threat. Sincere love encourages you and wants to help you flourish. When a man loves you, he is empathetic; when you hurt, he hurts. He is honest and faithful to you. He does not lie since he cares more about your feelings than his image or his ego. A man who loves you also trusts you. His love is not demonstrated by control or insecurity. He does not treat you like a possession but as an equal partner with valid physical and emotional needs. You do not belong to a man, but to God (Psalm 100:3 KJV). Love does not require you to be passive with no expectations of being treated with equal respect. A man who loves you respects your boundaries and does not expect you to always give in to his demands, but he is willing to compromise. A loving person loves himself.

Toxic Love is Not Genuine Love

A man who truly loves you does not exhibit the traits of an abuser. Abusive behavior is based on pride and selfishness. It is not love. Love does not harm you. In a healthy relationship, you can disagree with your partner without being attacked, humiliated, or ridiculed. Unlike a toxic relationship, a loving relationship allows you to openly and safely express your opinions.

Characteristics of Healthy Relationships

The equality wheel below exemplifies the characteristics of healthy relationships. Healthy relationships are safe and each person has power. Each person has an equal say and each person's needs are equally considered. Both partners are willing to compromise and one person is not catering to another person. Look at the equality wheel below.[25]

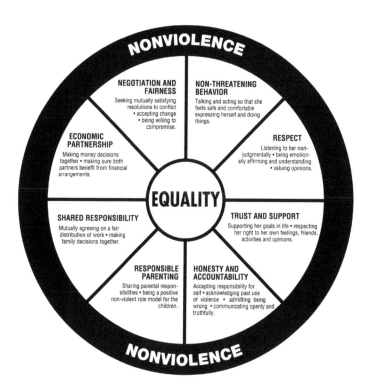

NONVIOLENCE

NEGOTIATION AND FAIRNESS
Seeking mutually satisfying resolutions to conflict • accepting change • being willing to compromise.

NON-THREATENING BEHAVIOR
Talking and acting so that she feels safe and comfortable expressing herself and doing things.

ECONOMIC PARTNERSHIP
Making money decisions together • making sure both partners benefit from financial arrangements.

RESPECT
Listening to her non-judgmentally • being emotionally affirming and understanding • valuing opinions.

EQUALITY

SHARED RESPONSIBILITY
Mutually agreeing on a fair distribution of work • making family decisions together.

TRUST AND SUPPORT
Supporting her goals in life • respecting her right to her own feelings, friends, activities and opinions.

RESPONSIBLE PARENTING
Sharing parental responsibilities • being a positive non-violent role model for the children.

HONESTY AND ACCOUNTABILITY
Accepting responsibility for self • acknowledging past use of violence • admitting being wrong • communicating openly and truthfully.

NONVIOLENCE

Wheel Gallery, www.theduluthmodel.org, © 2017 Domestic Abuse Intervention Programs, www.theduluthmodel.org/wheel-gallery

The Woman at the Well

In John 4 verses 4-26, John describes Jesus's encounter with a Samaritan woman at a well who had an unquenchable thirst for inauthentic love. When Jesus asked her for a drink, she initially questions Jesus. Jesus told her, "If you knew the gift of God, and who it is that asks you for a drink, you would have asked him and he would have given you living water" (John 4:10 NIV). The woman then asked Jesus to give her this water and Jesus tells her to call her husband. Jesus knew she had five husbands and was not married to the man she was with. She was astonished. Jesus then tells the woman that whoever drinks from this well will thirst again, "but whoever drinks the water I give them will never thirst" (John 4:7-16 NIV).

The story of the woman at the well teaches us that the things of this world, like love from a man, will never satisfy you. Like the water in the well, relationships with men will only temporarily satisfy your thirst for love. However, the love that Jesus offers is "living water." When you center your life on Jesus, His love will fill your heart so that you are not an empty vessel looking for love.

Traits of a Godly Man

A godly person possesses the fruit of the Holy Spirit. The nine attributes of the Holy Spirit are: love, joy, peace, long-suffering (patience), gentleness, goodness, faith, meekness, and temperance (self-control) (Galatians 5:22-23 KJV). These attributes exemplify how we should conduct ourselves and how we should treat one another. Someone possessing these fruit is not someone who will abuse you.

To recognize and appreciate the fruit of the Spirit, you must also possess the fruit of the Spirit. As you grow closer to God through prayer, meditation, and worship, you will recognize your true value and you will only desire a mate that complements your spiritual walk. The Bible instructs us to "seek ye first the kingdom of God, and his righteousness; and all these things shall be added unto you" (Matthew 6:33 KJV). The Holy Spirit gives you the ability to discern godly character traits, patience to wait on God's timing, and the ability to control yourself from making unwise choices.

Prayer:
Lord, reveal to me what healthy love looks like. Open my eyes so that I can see how perfect Your love is. Amen.

CHAPTER 3
RECOGNIZE DESTRUCTIVE PATTERNS

Scriptures

Ephesians 6:12 KJV: "For we wrestle not against flesh and blood, but against principalities, against powers, against the rulers of the darkness of this world, against spiritual wickedness in high places."

2 Corinthians 10:3-5 KJV: "For though we walk in the flesh, we do not war after the flesh: (For the weapons of our warfare are not carnal, but mighty through God to the pulling down of strong holds;) Casting down imaginations, and every high thing that exalteth itself against the knowledge of God, and bringing into captivity every thought to the obedience of Christ."

Recognize Your Patterns

Now that you can identify when a relationship or a person is destructive, the next step to overcoming destructive relationships is to determine whether you have developed a pattern of being in destructive relationships.

Signs You Have an Unhealthy Approach to Dating

Examine every relationship you were involved in since you started dating. Consider if any of the following are true:

- You've been in a series of unhealthy relationships or marriages.

- Your dating history is mainly defined by men who mistreat you, lie, cheat, or harm you.

- You date the same type of destructive person over and over.

- You seem to jump out of one bad relationship, right into another one.

- You've suffered serious financial loss because of a relationship.

- You've been married multiple times and your ex-spouse(s) are still alive.

- Drama and chaos in your relationships negatively impacted other areas of your life.

- Your relationships have negatively affected your children or other family members.

- You don't have healthy friendships outside of your relationships.

- Outside of dating relationships, people seem to walk all over you.

- Your relationships tend to be lopsided.

Your Role in Choosing Bad Partners

You have a role in who you allow in your life and the types of relationships you choose to be a part of. Who you allow into your life has a serious impact on you. Becoming self-aware and recognizing your tendency to pick the wrong people to be involved with is critical in overcoming abusive relationships.

Being in a relationship is a choice. All relationships require two people, even unhealthy ones. While you cannot directly control the actions of another person, you can control how careful you are in choosing your partners and how you respond when someone treats you poorly. You control how close someone can get to you and how much energy to give to someone. You control how quickly you become emotionally attached, and how long you remain in an unhealthy relationship.

Relationships can be unpredictable. It is likely that you did not know that someone you became romantically involved with would ultimately cause you pain. Most people would not willingly become involved with someone that they knew was abusive.

It is your primary responsibility to protect yourself and whatever you are responsible for from relationships that are harmful. Take time to carefully discern someone's character and pay close attention to any red flags that signal someone might be destructive. Be vigilant and approach relationships with a sober mind. Ephesians 5:15-16 ESV says to be careful how you walk, "not as unwise but as wise, making the best use of the time, because the days are evil."

Destructive Relationship Patterns are a Stronghold

Destructive relationship patterns signal a stronghold. The dictionary defines a stronghold as a well-fortified place, like a fortress or a castle.[26] Spiritually speaking, a stronghold is any "imagination" or "high thing that exalts itself against the knowledge of God" (2 Corinthians 10:5 KJV). In other words, a stronghold is anything that presents itself as stronger or more powerful than God.[27] We develop strongholds from defective thinking patterns based on lies and deception from the enemy.[28]

When a stronghold is presented in a person's life, the person perceives that the thing has complete power over them. A stronghold makes a person feel like they are hopeless. Sex and pornography, for instance, are strongholds for some people. For others, over-eating and alcohol can be a stronghold. All strongholds are destructive and often seem innocent at first. Many people who become dependent on drugs or alcohol do not start off as abusers. Many start using drugs infrequently or recreationally. Soon, the person's dependence on drugs overtakes them and wreaks complete havoc in their life, sometimes leading to death.

Abusive relationship patterns are also a stronghold. Specifically, the stronghold is codependency. Codependency refers "to people who feel extreme amounts of dependence on loved ones in their lives, and who feel responsible for the feelings and actions of those loved ones." [29] A codependent person is addicted to relationships, and forms "relationships that are one-sided, emotionally destructive, and/or abusive." [30]

Codependent people are people-pleasers and will serve others to their detriment. People who are codependent will go through enormous lengths to maintain a dysfunctional relationship. When relationships are so important that you tolerate being abused over and over again, or you are being disobedient to Christ, then you have made relationships your "god." You are seeking your validation, identity, and acceptance from a relationship rather than God. This is a form of idolatry and it is against God's will. The Word says that God is a jealous God, and you shall have no other God before Him (Exodus 20:3-4 KJV). Codependency is a stronghold.

The apostle Paul instructs us that "the weapons of our warfare are not carnal, but mighty through God to the pulling down of strong holds" (2 Corinthians 10:4 KJV). Your fight in overcoming destructive relationships is not against a person or even yourself. It is spiritual. The enemy, Satan, uses your weaknesses (i.e., your lack of awareness, need for validation, lack of moral support, fear, and lack of knowledge of who you are in Christ) to deceive you into relying on destructive relationships.

However, Paul says that when you accepted Jesus as your savior, God raised you up with Christ and seated you with Him in heavenly places (Ephesians 2:6). By doing so, God gave you power and authority over any stronghold, which the enemy must submit to. To use this power to overcome the enemy's schemes, you must know the truth, which is God's Word. In John 8:31-32 KJV, Jesus says to His followers, "If ye continue in my word, then are ye my disciples indeed; And ye shall know the truth, and the truth shall make you free." The way to break free from strongholds is to know God's Word and apply it against Satan's lies. The more familiar you are with God's Word and your identity in Christ, the more confident you are in asserting the power God gave you over the enemy's attacks. This is called spiritual warfare.

It is only by meditating, praying, and applying His Word that we can pull down strongholds. We cannot do this on our own. If we could, we would not need Jesus as our savior. First, acknowledge that you cannot overcome this stronghold on your own, and that you need God. Then, ask God to step in. Surrender to Him. The more time you spend in prayer and studying God's Word, the more your thoughts will align with His, making them obedient to Christ. By submitting to God and applying the power of His Word, you can take down the stronghold of codependent relationships, emotional strongholds, and generational curses of abuse.

Prayer:
Lord, reveal to me my unhealthy patterns in dating relationships. I acknowledge that I am powerless on my own to overcome the pattern of destructive relationships and I submit to Your will. Deliver me from the stronghold of codependent and abusive relationships. Amen.

CHAPTER 4
WHY ABUSE HAPPENS

Scripture

Proverbs: 29:25 KJV: "The fear of man bringeth a snare: but whoso putteth his trust in the Lord shall be safe."

Why Does This Keep Happening?

According to psychologists, there are several reasons why some people repeatedly enter into destructive, abusive relationships. People who consistently experience unhealthy relationships do so because they are not healthy. Unhealthy people seek and remain in relationships out of fear. To attract a great relationship, you must be in a good mental, emotional, and spiritual place as well.

Many people become involved in romantic relationships for the wrong reasons. Some people are seeking validation and acceptance from others. Some people seek relationships for support because they lack strong support of family and friends. Others use relationships for various provisions, like a place to live, food, or financial support. Some are lonely. All of these reasons touch on fundamental human needs that everyone must have and can be summed up into one main reason--they are depending on people for their needs instead of depending on God. Lack of adequate moral support or acceptance, feelings of rejection, and financial instability makes you a target for abuse. Consider some of the reasons you may have been systemically abused in your relationships.

1. You are Codependent

As mentioned before, if you are codependent you have an unhealthy dependence on relationships. Your identity is lost in other people's needs and desires. Your relationships are not reciprocal. You are a people-pleaser. You attempt to "rescue" your partners, or you need to be "rescued." If you are the more independent partner, then saving others from their problems gives you a sense of self-worth. You seek relationships where you are in control because it makes you feel safe. You think that by saving someone else, the person will value you more. Somewhere deep down, you don't feel you deserve someone of equal status. Due to being disappointed and neglected, I felt the need to control everything around me to protect myself. I was highly educated and had a good income, and I married an unstable man who was in and out of work and had poor finances. I was clearly the more independent and responsible person. But in a sense, I felt safe with him because he needed my help. I thought he would appreciate me more than others because I helped him.

If you are the one that needs saving, then you give too much power to other people. You don't take responsibility for your life choices due to your lack of confidence. You feel safer when other people are calling the shots. Codependent people place so much emphasis on relationships that they lack proper boundaries. Poor boundaries make you an easy target for being abused.[31, 32] Matthew 6:24 KJV says that "No man can serve two masters: for either he will hate the one, and love the other; or else he will hold to the one, and despise the other." If you are codependent, you have chosen man to be your master instead of God. This is not what God desires.

2. You Experienced Abuse as a Child

If you were abused or neglected as a child by your parents, you do not have a proper framework to make healthy relationship choices. You learned that abuse was normal and acceptable. Your boundaries were disregarded as a child, so you never learned to develop them.[33] If you were traumatized as a child due to abuse, you may settle for people you can dominate to protect you from being rejected or traumatized again. On an unconscious level, since you did not receive proper love and attention as a child, you do not feel worthy of being loved.

Prior to the tragic turn of events in my life that led me to start learning more about abuse, I did not know what boundaries were. I now realize that I tolerated abuse because I was not taught that I deserved to feel loved. We all need to feel loved and validated, especially from our parents. If your basic emotional needs for love, security, and validation were not met, you are likely to seek it in other places, like relationships. Your need to feel loved because of what you did not get as a child makes you more susceptible to abuse.

The Bible gives us hope. Psalm 27:10 KJV says that "When my father and my mother forsake me, then the Lord will take me up." When we accept Jesus as our Lord and Savior, He adopts us as His children. In Ephesians 1:5 NLT, Paul says that "God decided in advance to adopt us into his own family by bringing us to himself through Jesus Christ." God loves you more than any person ever will, even your parents.

3. You Have Poor Boundaries

Interpersonal boundaries define the limits you set on what you are willing to tolerate from others, and how your behavior impacts others. Boundaries separate what belongs to you and what does not belong to you. Healthy boundaries are essential to protecting yourself from the actions of destructive people. If you are consistently being abused, then your boundaries are too weak. Relational boundaries are more clearly discussed in chapter 6.

4. Poor Guidance

If you had no guidance or poor examples of relationships in your family, then you may not know what a healthy relationship looks like. If your parents were in abusive, dysfunctional relationships, then your model of relationships is dysfunctional. If you watched your parents tolerate abuse, or your parents neglected you for their relationships, you are prone to making unhealthy relationship choices as well. Generations of dysfunctional relationships can be so prevalent in your family, that your family normalizes and may even encourage abuse.

As a child, my parents were in numerous abusive relationships, placing more value on their relationships with other people than me and my siblings. I know my parents love me, but they simply were not capable of giving us the love or attention we needed as children. Because I did not understand the difference between a healthy and a dysfunctional relationship, I also endured numerous troubled relationships and many years of abuse of my own.

5. You Have Misplaced Values

We may be Christians, but we live in the world. Worldly values and lifestyles are the norm. Sadly, many Christians have conformed to a worldly lifestyle, and many of us choose to live outside of the will of God. The world's values about relationships between men and women are quite different from what God says. Worldly values encourage loosely entering into relationships without real commitment or serious consideration of the future consequences of your choices. Sexual immorality and casual relationships are considered acceptable to get our emotional and physical needs met. In the world, selfish needs come first.

However, if you choose to become emotionally involved with a man without discerning whether he can be a good spouse, or give your body to men you are not married to, then you have set yourself up for destruction. In Romans 12:2 KJV, Paul says, "be not conformed to this world: but be ye transformed by the renewing of your mind, that ye may prove what is that good, and acceptable, and perfect, will of God."

6. Loneliness or Rejection

Feeling lonely or rejected is a significant factor in allowing abusers into your life. When you are lonely, you are likely to seek companionship and validation from another person to feel good about yourself. Abusers are predators who prey on women who feel lonely or rejected. The abuser's kind words, shallow affection, and constant attention give you a much-needed boost of self-esteem. However, you don't have to rely on a man to feel accepted. You may be alone but you don't have to feel lonely. Isaiah 41:10 NIV, says that "So do not fear, for I am with you; do not be dismayed, for I am your God. I will strengthen you and help you; I will uphold you with my righteous right hand." God assures us that we are never alone.

Prayer:
Lord, I don't understand why I keep involving myself in the wrong relationships. Reveal to me the areas in my life that have affected my relationship choices as well as where my boundaries need strengthening. Amen.

CHAPTER 5
BE OBEDIENT

Scriptures

Deuteronomy 11:1 KJV: "Therefore, thou shalt love the Lord thy God, and keep his charge, and his statutes, and his judgements, and his commandments, always."

Psalm 1:1-3 KJV: "Blessed [is] the man that walketh not in the counsel of the ungodly, nor standeth in the way of sinners, nor sitteth in the seat of the scornful; But his delight [is] in the law of the LORD; and in his law doth he meditate day and night; And he shall be like a tree planted by the rivers of water, that bringeth forth his fruit in his season; his leaf also shall not wither; and whatsoever he doeth shall prosper."

Know His Commandments

To break free from destructive relationships, you must be obedient to God's commandments. To do this, you must study God's Word so that you understand what His commandments are. The Bible says that we perish for "a lack of knowledge" (Hosea 4:6 KJV). Psalm 119:11 KJV exclaims, "Thy word have I hid in mine heart, that I might not sin against thee." If you do not know what the Word says, then you are bound to behavior that will destroy you. Study God's Word daily and pray for guidance. Trust that God's ways are better than yours. John 15:7 ESV says, "If you abide in me, and my words abide in you, ask whatever you wish, and it will be done for you."

Surrender to Him

Surrender to God's will. To surrender you must acknowledge that on your own you are powerless over sin. Confess your sins, ask Him for forgiveness, and repent. It is God's desire to save us from destruction. John 3:16 KJV confirms this by saying that "For God so loved the world, that he gave his only begotten Son, that whosoever believeth in him should not perish, but have everlasting life." When you accept Christ as your Savior, the Bible says in Psalm 103:12 KJV, "As far as the east is from the west, so far hath he removed our transgressions from us." As believers, "there is therefore now no condemnation... in Christ Jesus" (Romans 8:1 KJV).

It is not God's desire for you to live in guilt and shame. Ask God to strengthen you in the areas that you are weak so that you can better serve Him. It is the power of the Holy Spirit, the same spirit that raised Jesus from the dead, that gives us the strength to overcome our sinful ways. Romans 8:11 declares that "if the Spirit of him that raised up Jesus from the dead" dwells in you, the Spirit that raised Christ from the dead shall also quicken your mortal body by the Holy Spirit that dwells in you!

Obey His Word

God's first commandment is to "love the Lord thy God with all thy heart, and with all thy soul, and with all thy mind, and with all thy strength." (Mark 12:30 KJV). God's second commandment is to "love thy neighbour" as you love yourself (Mark 12:31 KJV). Jesus says, "If ye love me, keep my commandments" (John 14:15 KJV). Obedience is your demonstration of your love for God and your faith (John 14:15).

Listen to the voice of the Holy Spirit for wisdom and discernment, and obey. The Bible tells us not to be conformed to this world, but to be transformed by the renewing of your mind (Romans 12:2). The Bible also instructs us to present our bodies as a living sacrifice, holy and acceptable unto God (Romans 12:1 KJV). As Christians, we are supposed to think and act differently from the rest of the world. The world advocates sex outside of marriage and lascivious behavior. However, follow God's commands, practice self-control, and abstain from sexual immorality. Avoid situations that may cause you to fall, which is a part of the enemies plan to wreak havoc in your life. The enemy's only goal is to "steal… kill… and destroy" (John 10:10 KJV).

Study and Pray

Meditate on God's Word daily and pray. Ephesians 5:26 KJV says, "That he might sanctify and cleanse it with the washing of water by the word." Spend time reflecting on Him and His goodness. Praise God for who He is and for all that

He has done for you. Thank Him even through your sufferings. Join a Bible-based church and attend regularly. It is important to participate in corporate worship (Hebrews 10:25 KJV). Surround yourself with others who support you and honor God's Word. Christian fellowship strengthens your faith and helps you to focus on God's desires and purposes for your life.

Even though we do not earn God's love, God promises that He will bless you for your obedience. God says in John 15:7 ESV, "If you abide in me, and my words abide in you, ask whatever you wish, and it will be done for you." God also promises that "if my people who are called by my name humble themselves, and pray and seek my face and turn from their wicked ways, then I will… heal their land" (2 Chronicles 7:14 ESV). Obedience demonstrates your faith and shows God that you trust Him. You will be surprised how living according to God's commands will miraculously change your life for the better. Developing a strong relationship with Christ and being obedient to God is a process. Even though we are saved from eternal death, the process of sanctification takes a lifetime. You will make mistakes and you will fall. However when you fall, confess, and get right back up.

Ask God for Wisdom

Ask God to reveal your mistakes and why you make them. Ask Him to show you the key character flaws in your partners that you missed. One of the roles of the Holy Spirit is to give you wisdom (2 Corinthians 12 KJV). Ask God to show you how these harmful people were able to slip into your life and earn your affection. Ask for revelation of your own character weaknesses that have contributed to your problems, and for discernment so that you can make better choices moving forward.

In your study and prayer time, also ask God to reveal what qualities you should be seeking in a life partner and how to go about the process of dating in a way that is pleasing to God. Be humble and willing to listen to all that He has to say. If you ask God, He will show you. With Christ, you have the capacity to change the trajectory of your relationships.

Continue to Abide in Him

God created us to be in relationship with Him. Continue to walk with God and seek His face. Without Christ, our lives are empty and incomplete. We are often searching for people to fulfill us in ways that only God can. Without a right relationship with Him, we seek to fill this void with carnal things like relationships, drugs, sex, and other destructive vices. God knew that we would be unable to live righteously without Him.

As you spend time with Him, He will show you things about yourself that you did not even know. Use the time you would normally spend in a relationship meditating on His Word. You cannot spend too much time with God. Talk to Him about all your problems and your feelings. The Bible tells us to cast our cares on Him, for He cares for us (1 Peter 5:7 KJV).

As your relationship with Christ grows, your faith grows. As your faith grows, He will strengthen you so that you are not desperate for the attention of a man to feel loved. You will be able to discern a harmful person from someone who is genuine. You will protect yourself better emotionally. You know that you are loved because God loves you, which is most important. You will become purpose-driven and not relationship-driven. Psalm 37:4 ESV says to "Delight yourself in the Lord, and he will give you the desires of your heart." At the right time, God will send you the person that He has in mind for you.

Additional Meditation Scriptures

John 14:15 KJV: "If ye love me, keep my commandments."

Joshua 1:8 KJV: "This book of the law shall not depart out of thy mouth; but thou shalt meditate therein day and night, that thou mayest observe to do according to all that is written therein: for then thou shalt make thy way prosperous, and then thou shalt have good success."

Prayer:

Lord, I desire to be more obedient to You and I acknowledge that I fall short. Please forgive me of my sins and strengthen me so that I can be more obedient to You. Show me where I am weak and where I am strong. Reveal to me sins that I am not aware of. Order my steps so that they are pleasing to You. Amen.

CHAPTER 6
ESTABLISH HEALTHY BOUNDARIES

Scripture

Matthew 7:6 KJV: "Give not that which is holy unto the dogs, neither cast ye your pearls before swine, lest they trample them under their feet, and turn again and rend you."

1. Healthy Boundaries Create Healthy Relationships

Learning to set proper boundaries is key to having healthy relationships. Boundaries distinguish what is rightfully yours and set limits on the treatment you tolerate from others. Healthy relational boundaries separate your needs from the needs of another person. Relational boundaries protect your body, your mind, and your emotions. They also ensure that you do not intrude on what is not yours. Boundaries are like a fence around a house. The fence establishes what belongs to the owner and protects the owner's property from intruders.

Similarly, having healthy boundaries protects you from the harmful actions of others. Having poor external relational boundaries is like opening your home to the public. It would not be safe to allow total strangers to walk into your home at will, sit on your couch, and sleep in your bed. More than likely, you have a door, which you keep locked, and maybe an intrusion alarm system.

By setting clear boundaries, you let others know what behavior is acceptable and what is not.[36] You are in control of setting your boundaries and it is your responsibility to let others know what they are. You should not assume that people know or should know your boundaries. While you may be considerate and respectful towards others, some people are not considerate. If your boundaries are poor, toxic people will use your kindness to walk all over you.

2. Types of Boundaries

There are different types of boundaries. They can be material, physical, mental, and emotional. All boundaries are important and serve a different function.

a. Material Boundaries

Material boundaries protect your possessions, like your money or your car. Choosing not to lend money to someone is a material boundary. If you loan someone money and give them a deadline to return it, then this is also a boundary.[34, 36]

b. Physical Boundaries

Physical boundaries protect your body and your personal space. For instance, when you tell someone that you do not want to be touched, or you do not want to have sex, that is a physical boundary. If someone touches you without your approval, that is a violation. Since you are responsible for your body, you must take measures to protect yourself from physical abuse or unwanted touching by someone else. A toxic person ignores your physical boundaries. If you consistently allow someone to touch you when you do not want to be touched, then your boundaries are weak.[34, 36]

Physical and sexual abusers disregard your physical boundaries and act as if they are entitled to your body or your space. This type of thinking is wrong because: 1) your body does not belong to them. 2) God created you; He put you in charge of your body. 3) You are not your own, but you were bought with a price (Corinthians 6:19). You are valuable to God. Your body is very important and you must live with the consequences for what happens to your body.

To implement healthy boundaries, protect yourself as the prized possession of God that you are. You are precious in God's eyes (Isaiah 43:4). You get to decide what you are comfortable with. Make your boundaries clear. Don't allow someone to pressure you into sex and do not give mixed signals. Don't allow someone to invade your privacy or your personal space. If something doesn't feel right, speak up or create distance between yourself and the other person.

c. Emotional Boundaries

Emotional boundaries protect your feelings and set limits on how you allow others to treat you. Healthy emotional boundaries prevent you from accepting blame for someone else's actions, "feeling guilty for someone else's feelings," or taking another person's "comments personally."[34] Healthy boundaries also protect the feelings of others, and prevent you from giving unwanted advice, blaming others for your problems, or being controlling.[34] When someone violates your emotional boundaries, it hurts your feelings. Not allowing someone to unfairly criticize and verbally abuse you is an emotional boundary. Other examples of setting emotional boundaries include: avoiding phone calls from a toxic person, not tolerating someone raising their voice, leaving a bad relationship, and telling someone that something he or she said was hurtful. There are many more ways to set emotional boundaries in relationships.

The Bible tells us to not give that which is holy to the dogs, and "neither cast ye your pearls before swine, lest they trample them under their feet, and turn again and rend you" (Matthew 7:6 KJV). Not every person deserves access to your heart or your feelings. Some people are not mature or responsible enough to handle your emotions with the care you deserve. The Bible also instructs us to diligently guard our heart, because "out of it are the issues of life" (Proverbs 4:23 KJV). When we don't properly guard our hearts, we set ourselves up for disappointment and heartache from others. It is not God's desire for you to repeatedly experience heartache from people who have no regard for you.

To implement healthy emotional boundaries, speak up when someone says or does something that hurts you emotionally. Be mindful about the information you share. Empathetic people, like me, tend to overshare because we naively assume that everyone has a great heart like us. When you don't set emotional boundaries, abusers can see this as a sign of weakness and the abuse will escalate. When someone disrespects your boundaries, clearly let them know and be ready to walk out of the relationship. A person who disrespects you is not someone you want to be around.

d. Mental Boundaries

Mental boundaries define your thoughts, beliefs, and opinions.[34, 36] Your ability to hold onto your opinions and beliefs and not be intimidated or swayed by someone else is a mental boundary.[34] Having healthy mental boundaries allows you to assert your own opinion, even when it is contrary to someone else's. A person who cannot accept your opinion without becoming angry does not respect your mental boundaries. If you frequently give in to the opinions of others to avoid confrontation, then your mental boundaries should be strengthened. On the other hand, if you are argumentative and unable to listen with an open mind, your boundaries are also weak.[34] Practice asserting your opinion if it is important. You can do this in a calm and clear way.[34] Be ready to walk away from people who cannot accept your opinion, without anger or irritation, when it is different from their own.

5. How to Set Healthy Boundaries
a. Practice Assertive Communication

If you struggle with poor boundaries you should practice assertive communication. Assertiveness is a skill that allows you to clearly communicate what your needs are and when your needs are violated.[35] Assertiveness allows you to communicate your feelings "directly and honestly," while being respectful to the feelings of the other person.[35] Being assertive does not require being aggressive, emotional, or rude. Contrary to assertive communication, passive aggressive behavior is "an indirect expression of hostility through procrastination, stubbornness," or "deliberate non-cooperation." [35] Passive-aggressive behavior is not assertive and is unhealthy.[35]

When you are not assertive, your confidence suffers. When your confidence suffers, so does your self-esteem. Self-esteem is your overall emotional evaluation of your own worth. Low self-esteem is a major contributor to many problems, including the need for validation from others. Low self-esteem encourages you to remain in abusive relationships. When you practice assertive communication, your confidence increases as well as your self-esteem. Confidence impacts the way that others treat you. [35]

Living to please others drains your resources and creates undue stress. People-pleasing does not minimize conflict, it adds conflict. Your time, energy, and resources are limited. You are human, and unlike God you cannot do everything or be everywhere. You must set limits on what you do for others to avoid it negatively impacting your well-being. Relentlessly giving to other people beyond what you are capable of leads to feelings of resentment.

Jesus was assertive. He said, no man takes my life from me, "but I lay it down of my own accord" (John 10:18 NIV). Jesus died on His own terms because He was the only perfect sacrifice who could restore our relationship with God, the Father. Jesus disagreed with the traditions of the Pharisees (Matthew 23; Luke 11:37-54; Mark 12:11-44; Luke 20:46-47) and overthrew the money changer's tables in the temple (Matthew 21:12) Jesus rebuked His beloved disciples at times (Luke 9:46-50) and there were occasions when He went alone to pray (Luke 5:16). Jesus challenged Satan in the wilderness (Matthew 4:4-11) and Jesus did not "go along with the flow" to please others.

b. Strive for Healthy Interpersonal Relationships

Jesus teaches us to have correct interpersonal relationships.[38] There arze times when conflict is necessary. Even though Jesus said to turn the other cheek, He does not want you to be a doormat. When people sense that your main goal in life is to please others, you will be taken advantage of. To be assertive, you must be okay with not being liked by others. Being well-liked by others is not a true measure of your worth. Some people who commit the most atrocious acts are popular and well-liked. Jesus was scorned by those He loved. No matter what you do, your actions will always rub someone else the wrong way. You are not called to be controlled by people or to conform to other people's opinions. God created you to be different.

c. Exercise Wisdom and Discernment

Implementing healthy boundaries requires wisdom. If you have codependent tendencies, then it is critical to realize that you are here to serve God and not man. Consider your motives before giving to someone. If you are giving purely out of generosity, then your giving is healthy. If you are giving so that others will like you, or out of obligation, then this is not healthy. 2 Corinthians 9:7 says that God loves a cheerful giver. Giving to be appreciated is especially unhealthy if it puts you in a bind. It is ok to take care of yourself.

Implementing boundaries requires practicing self-control. Not everyone deserves equal access to you. Different people should have different levels of significance in terms of your availability and your resources. If you are married, God comes first, then you and your spouse, then your children, and everyone else comes after that. If you are single, God comes first, then you, then your children if you have any, and then everyone else.

Pray for wisdom and discernment regarding who to let into your life, how close a person can get to you, how much you give to others, and generally how you let others treat you. Having wisdom and discernment is important in relationships because people are not always who they appear to be and sometimes they do not have the best intentions. Discernment allows you to see the truth behind people's actions. The more you nurture your relationship with God by meditating on His Word and obeying His commands, the more wisdom and insight you will have. The Holy Spirit empowers you with wisdom and discernment (1 Corinthians 2:12-14), and will guide you with setting appropriate boundaries. Listen to your gut instinct. That is the voice of the Holy Spirit inside of you.

Your personal experiences are also valuable when considering whether a person is helpful or destructive. Be mindful of behavior that mimics behavior of a destructive partner in your past. Learn to spot red flags and respond to them appropriately. Distinguish spending money, attention, and gifts from having good character.

d. Seek Professional Counseling

Professional counseling is another way to get help with setting appropriate boundaries. Psychologists, therapists, and licensed counselors are clinically trained to help you identify where your boundaries are weak and can help you implement boundaries to protect yourself and others. Counselors can also help you identify relationships that are detrimental and give insight regarding why you make certain choices. Get help from a Christian counselor that can give spiritual as well as academic insight. Talk to friends and family that you trust. It is difficult to see things clearly if you are being manipulated and have limited moral support from friends and family. Conversely, professional counselors help you to process your feelings without being influenced by someone else.

e. Practice Patience

Be patient when entering a relationship. Practicing patience requires self-discipline. The Bible teaches us that patience is a virtue (1 Corinthians 13:4; Ephesians 4:2; Colossians 3:12). Abusers are wolves in sheep's clothing. They are master manipulators and are good at pretending to be nice so that they can get what they want, even if it hurts you. Not every flattering tongue is coming from a pure place.

Proverbs 29:45 NKJV says that "a man who flatters his neighbor spreads a net for his feet."

The true test of a person's character is time. Do not rush into a relationship. When you rush into a relationship you miss important character flaws. A person looking for an easy target is generally not willing to put in the time or effort to earn your affection. When you are patient, you force your partner to earn your affection. Be patient with yourself. Developing healthy boundaries does not happen overnight and requires a lot of practice. You will become more comfortable at setting boundaries over time.

f. Practice Self-Control

Good boundaries require discipline. Practicing self-control makes you less vulnerable to toxic individuals. Self-control is a fruit of the spirit. Focus on serving God. The Bible says to "seek ye first the kingdom of God, and his righteousness; and all these things shall be added unto you" (Matthew 6:33 KJV). Spend time with God and be obedient to His laws. Take proper care of yourself and limit your exposure to bad company and environments that are contrary to a lifestyle that glorifies God. Abstain from sexual immorality. Avoid alcohol or any substance that alters your ability to think or to control yourself. The Bible instructs us to be sober and vigilant, "because your adversary the devil walks about like a roaring lion, seeking whom he may devour" (1 Peter 5:8 NKJV). Don't entertain relationships with ungodly men simply for attention and don't compromise your standards to avoid being alone. Don't let your emotions allow you to tolerate behavior that is not appropriate or does not line up with God's will. Jeremiah 17:9 KJV says, "The heart is deceitful… and desperately wicked." Therefore, put your trust in God's Word, not your feelings.

4. Why Are Boundaries Important?

It is important to have boundaries because you have a divine purpose and a calling to fulfill. God loves you and wants to use you. God uses people like you and me to fulfill His mission on Earth. Someone else is depending on what God has called you to do. Your future generations depend on you too.

Prayer:

Lord, I desire to have healthy relationships with others. Give me the courage and wisdom to know how to set better boundaries. Give me clarity on when to speak up and when to remain silent. Help me to not be influenced by people more than I should. Amen.

CHAPTER 7
AVOID SEXUAL IMMORALITY

Scriptures

1 Corinthians 6:18 KJV: "Flee fornication. Every sin that a man doeth is without the body; but he that committeth fornication sinneth against his own body."

1 Corinthians 6:13-15 NJKV: "Now the body is not for sexual immorality but for the Lord, and the Lord for the body. And God both raised up the Lord and will also raise us up by His power. Do you not know that your bodies are members of Christ?"

Sexual Immorality is Destructive

To break the yoke of destructive relationships, you must abstain from sexual immorality. Refraining from sex outside of marriage is probably the most important step to avoid toxic and abusive relationships. Sex outside of marriage is a sin (1 Corinthians 6:18).

God created us to be sexual beings, but He designed sex to be enjoyed between a husband and a wife in a marital covenant to seal the sacred union and to deepen intimacy. This strengthens families since children could be conceived. God recognizes sex within a marriage as "very good" (Genesis 1:31).

Sex outside of marriage is destructive. What God calls good, the enemy perverts. Not only does sex affect bodies, it deeply affects our emotions and our lives. Sex has serious spiritual consequences since the union created during sex occurs in the spiritual realm as well as the physical realm. During sexual intercourse, the Bible says, "The two will become one flesh" (1 Corinthians 6:16 NIV). We join ourselves emotionally, physically, and spiritually to whoever we have had sex with. When we go against God's will and have sex outside of marriage, we defile our temple, which is where the Holy Spirit resides. 1 Corinthians 6:18 NIV, urges us to "Flee from sexual immorality. All other sins a person commits are outside the body, but whoever sins sexually, sins against their own body." In Romans 8:6 KJV, Paul says "to be carnally minded is death." God's laws forbidding sex outside of marriage keep our temples pure and protect us from destroying ourselves.

Sexual immorality leads to all types of far-reaching harmful consequences, including: rejection, disease, children outside of wedlock, addictions, low self-worth, cycles of poverty, and sexual exploitation. You also lose your sense of identity when you give your body to sexual partners you are not married to.[39]

Sexual Immorality is Deceptive

Sex is powerful and serious. Abusers use sex to create a false sense of intimacy to lure and control victims. We are designed to crave intimacy. When you have sex with someone, you become connected to that person on the deepest level. You entrust this person with your emotions, your health, the possibility of conceiving a child, and other serious repercussions.

Sex outside of marriage leads to confusion. You are more easily deceived when you have sex with someone based on mere feelings and promises. Feelings generated after sex make you more trusting and will have you convinced that a person loves you when your connection is actually based on lust. Relationships based on lust are fleeting and allow a person to suddenly move on to another person, soon after spending tremendous amounts of energy in a relationship. Your self-worth is attacked when the connection you once thought was special turns out to be an illusion. Even though you physically bonded with that person and gave them your trust, there was no real commitment between you and the other person. The person you joined yourself to has no real responsibility to you.

Deception created between sexual partners can occur even if you and your partner have been exclusively involved for years. Unless you are married, you are still single. Without a marital covenant, any commitment you proclaim is merely words. You can be misled even if you marry the person you were sexually involved with. Therefore, it is important to abstain from sex until marriage so that you can better discern the other person's character.

Sin by its very nature is deceptive. Adam and Eve could eat from any tree in the Garden of Eden, but God specifically instructed them not eat from the Tree of Knowledge of Good and Evil (Genesis 3:3 KJV). The serpent told Eve that they would not die if they ate the fruit, but that their "eyes shall be opened," that they would become as gods, "knowing good and evil" (Genesis 3:5 KJV). The serpent deceived Adam and Eve by making them think that God didn't really mean that they would die, and he convinced them that they had very good reasons for eating the fruit. They knew it was against what God said, but they found a way to justify their actions; their eyes would be opened! The fruit didn't seem deadly, the fruit was enticing. Adam and Eve did not know that this one act of disobedience would cause the fall of mankind, would cause them to be kicked out of the Garden of Eden, and would permanently sever the relationship between man and God, until Jesus redeemed us.

The Bible says in Luke that when we hear and obey the words of Christ, it is like building our house with a foundation that is laid on a rock. On the other hand, when we choose not to hear and obey Christ, it is like building our house without a foundation on the earth (Luke 6:47-49 KJV). When the storms come, the house built on the rock will stand. The house built on the earth will fall and the ruin will be great.

Sex Outside of Marriage Devalues You

God created you in His image. God values you. Sex outside of marriage devalues you and lowers your self-esteem and your overall sense of self-worth. You are basically saying, I'm good to sleep with, but not worth marrying. Lack of sexual integrity allows your partners to define your worth and causes you to be confused about your identity in Christ. Being devalued by others leads to depression, robs you of peace, creates feelings of insecurity, and opens the door to other destructive behaviors. Moreover, sin separates us from God and allows the enemy to stir up feelings of guilt and shame.

For many years, my identity was wrapped up in my romantic partners. I did not realize it at the time, but my various romantic encounters were taking a serious emotional toll on me. Although I was able to achieve high levels of success professionally and academically, I allowed men to take advantage of me and I was repeatedly disappointed. I lost touch with who I was and I had no idea that my unique gifts were significant to God. I made myself small to please others and did not think that God had a special plan for me. I had been hurt so many times, I became emotionally detached, and I learned to keep one foot in the door and one foot out of the door with anyone I was involved with.

Sex Makes You Emotionally Vulnerable

To have sex you must make yourself vulnerable on some level, and you form an intense bond with that person that can be addictive and difficult to break. Your body releases hormones like oxytocin that makes you intensely desire that person.[40] This is why it is hard to leave a relationship once you've been intimate, even when you know the person is not good for you. Often, the illusions in your mind after sex are the only thing keeping a relationship together, especially an abusive one. If you never have sex with an abuser, the abuser is not as attractive and his pull is not very strong.

It's easy to fall into sexual sin but it is difficult to mend your heart, be a single parent, manage a disease, or pick up the pieces of your life after you've been messed over by someone. God did not create you to have emotional attachments to numerous people you've slept with. The bonds created during sex are strong and cause significant pain when the relationship takes a turn for the worse.

Waiting Exposes Character

The problem with having sex before marriage is that you don't really know the person's true character. The person you meet initially is often not the person you think they are. Character flaws can be camouflaged when someone is trying to impress you. Even when you become married you are still learning things about your new spouse.

Refraining from sex strengthens your ability to discern the difference between someone who seems good and someone who is good. By preserving yourself until marriage, you can clearly see if a person really cares about you or simply what you can do for them. By maintaining sexual integrity, your mind is sober, and you are not swept away by a man's smooth talk or chivalrous acts. Time is the best indicator of whether a man is trustworthy, or if he has major character issues. Over time, an abuser's mask will slip, revealing his true character. If a man loses interest in you because you will not have sex, then count it a blessing.

Abstaining Reveals Selfish Motives

Abstaining from sex also wards off men with selfish motives. A man seeking to gratify his flesh wants convenience. A selfish person wants you because of what he can get from you, not what he can give. This could be your body, your affection, your resources, or even social status. An abuser's motives are selfish. When a selfish person cannot get what he wants, he will leave you alone and he will find another person to get his needs met. This is why a person pressuring you into sex or anything else a definite red flag. Love is patient and is not self-seeking. A selfish man is thinking of himself; he is not thinking of the consequences of engaging in sex or how sex will impact you.

It is your job to protect yourself from men who want sex and loyalty but cannot commit themselves to you in marriage. Having sex with someone you are not married to is like carefully constructing a beautiful mansion and then allowing a total stranger to come into your home and vandalize it. The stranger can trash your house, rob you, and then abandon it without a care. The stranger made no investment and is not obligated to care for your property. He isn't concerned about how much you saved or how hard you work to maintain it.

You are far more valuable than any mansion. You were handcrafted by God and you are His workmanship. Unlike material things, you cannot be replaced. When you have sex outside of marriage, you are offering all that you have to a person who has not earned the treasure inside of you.

Intimate Relationships are Difficult to Leave

The attachments formed during sex make it harder to leave a relationship than if you have never been intimate. Many relationships and marriages are formed that would not exist if sex had never occurred. Unhealthy attachments lead to unhealthy relationships, which lead to unhealthy marriages, and potentially divorce. Also, finding strength to leave an unhealthy relationship is exacerbated when you conceive a child with an abuser. Once a child is conceived, the relationship is taken to a new level. There is a new life that you both are responsible for, and this connection will be for a lifetime. Even worse is that an abusive person cannot be a good lover or a good parent. When you have a child with a person who is abusive, you put you and your child at risk for being hurt or neglected. It is all too common that one parent kills the other parent and his or her children, or an abuser, like a boyfriend, kills the child of the person with whom he was involved. In the case that the abuser is the biological father of the child, it is very difficult to prevent him from seeing the child since state laws are designed to encourage a relationship with both parents. Even with some protection from the court, the abuser will be a parent to your child forever, and if the child is prevented from having a relationship with the other parent, the child will be hurt by that missing connection.

Sometimes women think that once a child is born, an abuser's behavior will change for the better. However, a person's character will not change because you conceive a child together. You cannot expect a person to be a faithfully committed family man when he never demonstrated the maturity to be a faithful lover. Actions speak louder than words, so despite an abuser's empty promises, it is unlikely that an immature man will suddenly be responsible towards you or your children.

You Are Worth the Wait

True love is marked by real commitment. If a man truly loves you, he will commit to you in marriage before having sex. A man who does not want to commit to you in marriage is not worthy of having your body. Marriage is a lifelong commitment that requires a high level of spiritual maturity, responsibility, and tremendous sacrifice. There are serious spiritual, legal, and financial repercussions when you become married to someone. God desires marriage to reflect him and He sets very high standards about how spouses are to love each other. God commands spouses to be fully submitted to one another in a marriage. Ephesians 5:25 says a husband is to love his wife the way Christ loves the church. Christ loved the church so much that He gave His life.

God's laws are not to limit you from expressing yourself, but to protect you from serious harmful consequences. By abstaining from sexual immorality, you make better relationship choices and you are more emotionally stable. Your overall sense of self-worth increases and you can embrace your own identity, apart from a relationship. Accordingly, you won't tolerate abusive behavior to be in a relationship. You are happy and whole as a single person.

You Can Overcome with Help from God

It is not easy to stop having sexual relationships when fornicating has become your norm. It is possible to become addicted to the power and pleasure of sex. Your flesh is constantly at war with the Spirit. Galatians 5:17 KJV says that "the flesh lusteth against the Spirit, and the Spirit against the flesh: and these are contrary the one to the other: so that ye cannot do the things that ye would." Paul also exclaims, "For if you live according to the flesh, you will die; but if by the Spirit you put to death the misdeeds of the body, you will live" (Romans 8:13 NIV).

The power to live a sexually pure lifestyle requires the power of the Holy Spirit. The same Spirit that raised Jesus up from the dead has the power to strengthen your body to refrain from sin. This is the Holy Spirit, and it is a gift from God. Once you become a born again believer, the Holy Spirit dwells inside of you. When you received His Spirit, your old man died to sin, and it is Christ inside of you that is living. Paul says, "I am crucified with Christ: nevertheless I live; yet not I, but Christ liveth in me: and the life which I now live in the flesh I live by the faith of the Son of God, who loved me, and gave himself for me" (Galatians 2:20 KJV). Christ was perfect, He never sinned. Jesus's death and resurrection conquered sin and death for all who believed on Him.

To have victory over sin you must build up your spirit man. To do this, you must develop an intimate relationship with God by studying His Word, praying, and obeying His commandments. You also strengthen the spirit by starving your flesh. Jesus said, "Watch and pray so that you will not fall into temptation. The spirit is willing, but the flesh is weak" (Matthew 26:41 NIV). The Holy Spirit gives you the power to overcome sin and helps us in our times of weakness (Romans 8:26 NIV).

The Holy Spirit is God and has various important functions and roles. It bears witness for us, helps our infirmities, and makes intercession for us (Romans 8:16 KJV; Romans 8:26 KJV). The Holy Spirit enables you to understand and interpret God's Word (John 16:13 KJV). It gives you peace, comforts you, and assures you by bringing into remembrance all that God has done (John 14:16, KJV; John 14:26 KJV). It is the Holy Spirit that equips you with spiritual gifts for the edification of God's kingdom. It is the power of the Holy Spirit that allows you to control your anger and gives you the ability to forgive others. The Holy Spirit accomplishes God's purpose on the earth (1 Corinthians 12:4-12 KJV; Ephesians 4:11-12 KJV).

God knows that we cannot avoid sin in our own strength. If we had the power to conquer sin on our own, then Jesus would not have had to die. Therefore, it is only when we are submitted to Christ and walking in the Spirit, not our flesh, that the power of the Holy Spirit can strengthen us.

Additional Meditation Scriptures

Romans 8:6 KJV: "For to be carnally minded is death; but to be spiritually minded is life and peace."

Romans 6:12-13 KJV: "Let not sin therefore reign in your mortal body, that ye should obey it in the lusts thereof. Neither yield ye your members as instruments of unrighteousness unto sin: but yield yourselves unto God, as those that are alive from the dead, and your members as instruments of righteousness unto God."

1 Thessalonians 4:3-5 NIV: "It is God's will that you should be sanctified: that you should avoid sexual immorality; that each of you should learn to control your own body in a way that is holy and honorable, not in passionate lust like the pagans, who do not know God."

1 Corinthians 6:19-20 NIV: "Do you not know that your bodies are temples of the Holy Spirit, who is in you, whom you have received from God? You are not your own; you were bought at a price. Therefore honor God with your bodies."

Galatians 5:17 KJV: "For the flesh lusteth against the Spirit, and the Spirit against the flesh: and these are contrary the one to the other: so that ye cannot do the things that ye would."

Romans 12:1 KJV: "I beseech ye therefore, brethren, by the mercies of God, that ye present your bodies a living sacrifice, holy, acceptable unto God, which is your reasonable service."

Matthew 5:27-28 KJV: "Ye have heard that it was said by them of old time, Thou shalt not commit adultery: But I say unto you, That whosoever looketh on a woman to lust after her hath committed adultery with her already in his heart."

Prayer:

Heavenly Father, I am weak in the area of sexual immorality. I acknowledge that my body is a temple. Forgive me for any impure thoughts or actions that are sexually immoral. Fill me with Your Spirit so that I may control my flesh. I cannot do this on my own. Help me make better choices so that I may avoid temptation. Amen.

CHAPTER 8
MAXIMIZE YOUR TIME ALONE

Scripture

Isaiah 41:10 KJV: "Fear thou not; for I am with thee: be not dismayed; for I am thy God: I will strengthen thee; yea, I will help thee; yea, I will uphold thee with the right hand of my righteousness."

Take Time Away from Dating

If you have experienced a destructive relationship or a failed marriage, take time away from dating. It is important to spend time by yourself to reflect on your experiences and your goals. Ask yourself why you entered into each failed relationship or marriage and pray for clarity. This time alone gives you an opportunity to meditate on your choices and examine why you made them. It is also a chance to get real about where you are in life and what you want. Ask God what you can change so that your life can be better.

Take an inventory of your current emotional and mental state, physical health, finances, professional progress, and other responsibilities. Consider the health of your relationships with your children (if you have them), family, and others. Consider the strength of your support system.

Spend Time Working on You

When I thought about the time, energy, resources, and affection I wasted on relationships that yielded nothing but pain and misery, I realized that having toxic friends and men in and out of my life was not worth it. I can never get that time back. You can never get your time back.

Do you know what your gifts and talents are? Do you have any hobbies? Use this time to develop areas in your life where you are underutilizing your gifts. You have an identity and talents to offer outside of your relationships and outside of being a friend, a mother, a spouse, a girlfriend, or a loving family member.

Spend time strengthening the areas where you are weak. If you lack confidence, start taking risks. Challenge yourself to get out of your comfort zone. Consider group classes to improve your self-esteem, learn a new skill, or grow in other areas. Work on your physical health. If you are unhappy with where you are physically, consider making the appropriate changes to get into better physical shape. Start working out and change your diet.

Make a list of the qualities you are seeking in a mate and compare it to your qualities. If you want someone who is financially stable, you should be financially stable. If you want someone spiritually minded, you should be spiritually minded. If you want someone with their stuff together, you should have your stuff together. On the other hand, if you have a long list of things you bring to the table, don't lower your standards to be in a relationship. Only date someone whose values and lifestyle align with yours. Don't settle for less than what you are.

Avoid getting into a relationship until you have healed emotionally, and you are mentally and financially stable. When you are in a healthy place in these areas, you can make healthy relationship choices. When you are not in a good place in any of these areas, you are needy and you seek to get your needs met in someone else. Other people are not Jesus. They cannot save you. It is God's desire for you to enter a relationship whole, not depending on someone else to validate you.

Coping with Loneliness

God created each of us with a void, an emptiness that only He can fill. Loneliness is an indication of this void and it is our signal to get closer to God. We were created to be in a relationship with Him. God loves to be intimate with you and He wants to be the center of your attention.

Relationships with men can give you temporary comfort but cannot provide you with the sense of fulfillment or joy that only God can give. The Samaritan woman at the well was not alone, yet she was unfulfilled. Jesus reminds us that we can have relationships and still be unfulfilled, but if you drink the water of His well, you will never thirst again. Jesus said, "I am the bread of life: he that cometh to me shall never hunger; and he that believeth on me shall never thirst" (John 6:35 KJV). Jumping from person to person, relationship to relationship, city to city, job to job, or church to church will not make you happy. Peace comes from the Lord (John 14:27 NIV).

Without an intimate relationship with God, our life is empty and without meaning. God designed us to have needs that cannot be solved by family, relationship status, social status, wealth, education, or looks. You don't know other people's struggles. Some of the richest and most accomplished people are very depressed and lonely. Many marriages that look perfect on the outside are empty on the inside. The most successful people are often the most misunderstood.

Develop Yourself Spiritually

God often uses periods of loneliness and isolation so that you can accomplish His purpose. When you are alone, you have more time to meditate on His Word, seek His direction, and dedicate yourself to fulfilling your purpose. You also get to understand your identity in Christ, and what gifts you have to offer. Many people go through their whole lives without knowing their purpose and how valuable their gifts are to the kingdom.

The Bible states that God knew us before we were in our mother's womb. God knew what He wanted you to accomplish before the foundation of the world. God wants to show you who He created you to be and what you have inside of you. You were not created to be a bystander to everyone else's pursuits. You were not created to watch everyone else shine while you settle for mediocrity. You have gifts that are valuable to the kingdom.

Take Time to Heal

God also uses our lonely periods to heal us from past wounds. God wants to restore you and wants you to know how much He loves you. Spending time alone with God allows you to develop a much greater appreciation for Him. You will learn to hear His voice and you will also learn what is not coming from God. The more time alone you spend with Him, the more the spirit inside of you strengthens so that you are less likely to entertain voices that want to discourage you. The enemy is against you fulfilling your purpose to glorify God. The voice of the enemy tells you that it's too late to achieve your purpose. The enemy wants you to live in guilt and shame because of past mistakes. While God chastises those He loves, He is full of compassion. He does not want you to live in a state of condemnation. Pray to God for strength in this area. Read His Word, meditate with Him daily, and live by His principles. Use your time alone to take an inventory of your life now and where you want to be.

Ask God for Direction

Along with working on yourself, ask God for help. God can use you to help other people in need. Ask God to connect you with people to help you with your journey. Ask God to remove the wrong people from your life. At the right time, God will send people and resources to help you fulfill His purpose. Asking God to send the right people gives you a healthier support system, making you less susceptible to relying on destructive relationships. Ask God for patience and for increased faith during your period alone. In turn, you can encourage other people that you would not have been able to help if you were not alone. Get active in church and volunteer in your community. Serve in a food pantry or women's shelter, help the poor, minister to children, or serve in any other outreach activity. Helping others is very rewarding and helps you cope with feeling lonely. Serving others less fortunate than you teaches you to be more grateful. There is someone who would love to be in your shoes.

Ask God for Revelation

Ask God to reveal what a healthy relationship looks like so that you can detect people who are not right. Let Him teach you what love looks like, even if you didn't have good examples. God will show you what it means to be faithful and never-failing. God's love is perfect. God is consistent. If you look back on your life, you will see how good God really is. The more you meditate, you will not want to disappoint Him because you will gain a greater appreciation of who He is and all that He has done. You will see how God has had His hand over your life since you were born.

Devote Your Affection to Him

Paul instructs us to present our bodies as a living sacrifice. God commands us to love the Lord God with all our heart, all our soul, and all our mind (Matthew 22:37 KJV). God wants our hearts, our devotion, and our trust. The Bible says without faith, it is impossible to please God. Faith is the substance of things hoped for, the evidence of things not seen. Faith is marked by action. When we trust God and do things His way, despite our circumstances and despite being discouraged by others, we are demonstrating our level of faith.

As you spend more time with Him, you will become so consumed with His love and His goodness that He is the most important thing in your life. You will become less concerned with relationships with men and more concerned with pleasing Him. No person can be as good to you as He can, not even you.

Let God Use You

As you develop an appreciation for Him and begin living for Him, He will bless you. After my experiences, I decided to put my trust in God, and He has opened doors for me that I did not think were possible. Jesus instructs us to seek first the kingdom of God, and all these things will be added unto you. We seek His kingdom by having faith, striving to be obedient, studying His Word, and praying continually. God will use your alone time to prepare you for a life that is better than you can imagine. He will use your time alone to prepare the wonderful spouse He has for you.

Trust God's timing. By trusting God and waiting on His timing, you will be ready for a relationship, spiritually and emotionally, when the time comes. You will be at a stable place in life, not looking for outside love, and ideally you will be walking in your purpose. Your future spouse will recognize you for the wonderful woman of God that you are and will appreciate how God is using you to advance His kingdom. While you may feel alone at times, God says to fear not, for He is with you. There are people out there waiting for what you have to offer and who need to hear your story.

Prayer:

Single Ladies

Lord, thank you for never leaving me. There are times when I am lonely. Comfort and assure me so that I am not looking for love outside of You. During this time alone, help me to know more about myself. Show me the areas in my life that I need to work on. Prepare me for the spouse You have for me. Amen.

Married Ladies

Lord, thank you for never leaving me. I really need You right now. I feel alone and rejected in my marriage. Comfort me so that I can continue to honor You, and so that I do not fall into temptation. There are times that I do not know what to do. Give me Your peace and Your wisdom. Amen.

CHAPTER 9
ACCEPT YOUR EXPERIENCES

Scripture

2 Corinthians 12:9 KJV: "And he said unto me, My grace is sufficient for thee: for my strength is made perfect in weakness. Most gladly therefore will I rather glory in my infirmities, that the power of Christ may rest upon me."

Accept Your Experiences

Accept your past experiences. Whether you were habitually abused, cheated on, walked over, or lied to, your experiences are real. Your pain is real. Someone you cared for hurt you. Allow yourself time to grieve. It does not matter who they are, you do not deserve being mistreated. Accepting your pain does not make you weak, instead it acknowledges that you are human and helps you grow. Pain is an indication that something is not right and pretending something didn't happen does not help you make better future choices.

Accept if you did not really know the person or what you were getting yourself into. Accept that you were deceived. Accept that you don't understand why certain people mistreat you. Embrace the difficulties of your childhood experiences and how they may have contributed to your poor relationship choices. Acknowledge if you grew up in a home that was far less than perfect, or if you were neglected by either of your parents. Accept if people weren't there for you like you needed them to be. Accept if you have abused others. Accept your experiences, and that you tried your best. People are not perfect. They neglected or abused you because of their issues. You did not cause someone to mistreat you.

Recognize Your Mistakes

Recognize your contributions to your experiences. No one forces you to be in a relationship, even if they try to. A relationship takes two people. Consider whether you rushed in or ignored several red flags. Consider if you willingly engaged in sexual immorality and how this may had led to poor judgment. Admit if your motives were unhealthy, like you needed a place to live, were in financial distress, or some other reason. Acknowledge if you were vulnerable from a previous relationship and you jumped into a new relationship to ease the pain. Consider whether your priorities were misplaced, and you put more time and energy into trying to please a man than spending time with God. Confess if you were impatient or too trusting.

The step of acknowledging your contributions and shortcomings is absolutely critical in overcoming the cycle of destructive relationships. By recognizing your role and your weaknesses, you are no longer a victim of your circumstances. Recognizing your weaknesses puts you in the driver's seat. When you know what your vulnerabilities are, you can make better decisions about your approach to relationships. When you acknowledge that you don't have it all together, it opens the door for God to come into your heart to comfort and guide you. Remember that in the parable of the prodigal son, the younger son asks his father for his portion of his inheritance, leaves his father's presence, and squanders it. Eventually the son has nothing and is forced to eat with the swine to prevent starvation. The son ultimately runs back to his father after coming to his senses. The father does not turn his back on his son, but rather gives him the best robe, a ring, and a magnificent feast. Just as the forgiving father embraced his son after his son carelessly walked away, God will also embrace you. As demonstrated in the book of Hosea, God is forever married to the backslider.

No matter what happened to you or what you did, Jesus knows how you feel and He cares. God does not desire for you to be habitually abused. You must accept your experiences so that God can teach you what is right from what is wrong. For those of us who grew up witnessing or experiencing abuse, God must reprogram the way that we think about relationships and how we should be treated. He will show you how you should be loved.

You Are Responsible for Your Life

Your life is a reflection of your choices and the choices you make have consequences. Be vigilant and stay strong in your faith. Be encouraged. Don't let anyone downplay your experiences. Your experiences are not identical to anyone else's, so disregard when people try to compare their experiences to yours. Also, do not compare yourself to another person. Focus on your own journey. Just because someone handled their experiences differently does not make you better than or less than them.

Your personal growth is not a competition. Recovery is a process. It may take many years and more than a few church services to heal from your past. If we were able to fix ourselves, we would not need Christ. Christ instructs us to cast our burdens on Him, because His yoke is easy and His burden is light.

Seek Professional Help

Seek professional counseling if you can. The counsel of a qualified, caring professional can help you see things from another perspective. This person should be a strong Christian, having spiritual and academic insight. If you cannot afford professional counseling, seek a support group at church or another organization. Read literature on healthy relationships, setting boundaries, and other topics that give you biblical insight.

Prayer:

Heavenly Father, help me to accept my experiences for what they are. The pain of my past is too much for me to bear. Help me to let go of my past. Teach me so that I can use my experiences to make better choices. Help me to cast my cares onto You, because You care for me. Amen.

CHAPTER 10
FORGIVE OTHERS

Scriptures

Matthew 6:14-15 KJV: "For if ye forgive men their trespasses, your heavenly Father will also forgive you: But if ye forgive not men their trespasses, neither will your Father forgive your trespasses."

Control Your Anger

It is normal to experience anger for being mistreated. I did not realize how angry I was until after a series of very traumatic experiences, including a nearly fatal miscarriage, after which I was alone with God. For three years after my divorce, I was still very angry at my ex-spouse for mistreating me. I was angry at every person in my past that deceived me after I trusted them and gave to the point of neglecting myself. I was mad at the people from church who did not listen to me when I was speaking up about my marriage. I was mad that people from church disregarded my cries for help, did not believe me, and were advising me to stay in a marriage that nearly wrecked my life. I was mad that my own family did not believe me when I admitted how I was being mistreated. But mostly, I was mad at myself for allowing this to happen.

I was angry at the doctors for not taking me seriously and dropping the ball when I told them that something was not right with my child. I was angry because although I went to every appointment, and sought medical treatment when I was in labor, their recklessness led me to the emergency room where I had to fight for my life. I was mad that I lost my baby, the person that mattered the most and the only person I had left. I was mad that even though I was kind to others, others did not return that same level of kindness. I was mad at friends who belittled me and relatives who mistreated me. I was mad at my parents for not being there for me and not showing the love I needed as a child.

I had no idea how much anger was inside of me. I looked normal on the outside and I treated others very well, but on the inside I was boiling hot. I was so angry after the accumulation of those experiences that I could have set the world on fire. My anger had turned to rage. I was like gasoline without a match. Anything could have sent me completely over the edge. Only the grace of God kept me from losing my mind. I underwent eight weeks of a group anger management class and I now realize that maybe God had to isolate me for a period of time to protect me and others.

But anger is normal. God does not tell us to not be angry. Jesus showed great anger when He overturned the tables of the money changers and the dove-sellers in the temple (Matthew 21:12-13 KJV). But God does tell us not to sin when we are angry. For instance, thoughts of harming someone is sinful. He instructs us to control our anger by not letting the sun go down upon our wrath, nor give place to the devil (Ephesians 4:26-27 KJV). God further instructs us to put away all bitterness, wrath, anger, clamour, and evil speaking in Ephesians 4:31 KJV.

The Bible says don't allow anger and malice to give a foothold to the enemy. Holding on to anger gives the enemy a chance to encourage us to go against God and take matters into our own hands. Satan comes to steal, kill, and destroy (John 10:10 KJV). The enemy loves strife and he likes it when you are bitter. When we let anger consume us, we seek revenge. But God tells us not to avenge ourselves, but to "leave room for God's wrath," because vengeance belongs to God and He will repay (Romans 12:19 NIV). The Bible assures us to not be deceived, for "God is not mocked: for whatsoever a man soweth, that shall he also reap" (Galatians 6:7 KJV). It is not your job to repay others for what they did to you. Acting on your feelings brings you down along with them. God is much better at dealing with people who hurt you than you will ever be. Instead, pray for them.

You Must Let Go

Holding on to the past is destructive. Paul tells us to forget those things which are behind and reach forward to those things which are ahead (Philippians 3:13 KJV). Lot's wife turned into a pillar of salt when she looked back to the city of Sodom against the explicit warnings of God's angels. Lot's wife was consumed with her identity in Sodom; she could not see her value outside of it (Genesis 19:10-26 KJV).

It can be hard to let go of your past when you have been repeatedly let down by others or when you don't see your own worth outside of what you had. Sometimes it's hard to let go when you have experienced significant pain and hardships, because pain is familiar to you. You may deliberately hold on to pain because you don't believe you have an identity outside of your painful experiences. Like me, you may even be afraid of success because success takes you out of your comfort zone and may bring resentment and pain. You may sabotage yourself to fit in a box because you are afraid of being rejected if you climb out of it. I believe many of us know what we can do to place ourselves in a better position, but we are afraid to do it. We'd rather suffer and be comfortable than thrive and be uncomfortable. God wants you to experience joy and peace on Earth. Your experiences do not define you, but are simply to help you grow to encourage someone else. You are far more than your experiences, who hurt you, or who left you. Your future is far more significant than your past.

Forgive Those Who Hurt You

Forgive those who hurt you. Colossians 3:13 KJV tells us to forbear and forgive one another, just as Christ forgave us. God wants us to show mercy to others just as He has shown mercy to us. I had to learn to forgive my parents and anyone else from my past. Now, I'm learning to quickly forgive others when they hurt me. I'm also learning to have compassion and to see the pain in others that resulted in their behavior towards me. One of the steps I took that helped me get past my anger was to write a letter to my ex-lover, my ex-husband, and a few other people who betrayed me. In each letter, I forgave them and asked for forgiveness for anything I did. I did this despite the fact that I treated them well and did nothing to deserve being abused.

Forgiving others does not mean that you are accepting their wrong actions as okay. Forgiveness also does not mean that you forget what happened. It means that you are no longer holding this person accountable for what they did to you. Your act of forgiveness is a demonstration of obedience to God. Forgiveness is not for the person you forgive; it is to free you so that you can move on with your life. Remember, God loves this person too.

Ask the Holy Spirit for wisdom. Reconcile relationships only if possible. Just because you forgive someone, does not mean they should be in your life. Toxic people should be kept at a distance. If a person is unrepentant, then reconciliation is not possible. You know a person is repentant because they acknowledge your feelings and their behavior permanently changes. The Bible says if a person who wronged you hears you and repents, then you have regained a friend Matthew 18:15 KJV. However, if a person is not sorry or chooses not to repent, forgive them anyway and move on with your life.

Be willing to let go or distance yourself from all unhealthy relationships, including your family if necessary. Distancing yourself from family does not mean that you don't love them, it just means that you care more about your well-being than pleasing them. You may have to accept that you will lose a lot of people. Moreover, some of them may never understand how their actions have harmed you.

Forgive Yourself

Finally, you must forgive yourself for the choices that you made. If God can forgive you, so should you. Jesus was crucified so that we don't have to carry around the weight of our sins. Romans 8:1 KJV declares that when you accept Christ as your Savior, there is "now no condemnation to them which are in Christ Jesus." God does not want us to walk around in shame, guilt, and bitterness. He does not want us to be burdened with making mistakes, taking the responsibility for other people's problems, and carrying the weight of the world. Instead, we are to take His yoke upon us and learn from Him, because His yoke is easy and His burden is light (Matthew 11:30). Only Christ is strong enough to bear our shortcomings and our afflictions. In Christ you are no longer bound to your painful experiences or your sins! You are free. He who the Son sets free is free indeed.

Additional Meditation Scriptures

Ephesians 4:26-27 KJV: "Be ye angry, and sin not: let not the sun go down upon your wrath: Neither give place to the devil."

Proverbs 29:8 KJV: "Scornful men bring a city into a snare: but wise men turn away wrath."

Prayer:

Lord, thank you for forgiving me. Help me to forgive those who hurt me. Help me to forgive myself. Please forgive me for not showing the mercy to others that You showed me. Give me discernment to know who should remain in my life, and who should not remain in my life. Amen.

CHAPTER 11
DATE WITH A PURPOSE

Scripture

2 Corinthians 6:14 KJV: "Be ye not unequally yoked togeth-er with unbelievers: for what fellowship hath righteousness with unrighteousness? and what communion hath light with darkness?"

Change Your Dating Habits

Living a godly lifestyle requires discipline and a change in your habits. Instead of casually entertaining various men that you may be attracted to, date with a purpose. You should only date a man who is centered in Christ and that you would consider marrying.

It is important to establish proper boundaries when entering romantic relationships to protect your body, your spirituality, and your emotions. Your boundaries make you much less likely to be harmed by someone who does not have good motives. Your boundaries also send a message that your body and your feelings are very important. The goal is to avoid becoming too intimately involved until you know his true character, what his intentions are, whether he is trustworthy, and whether his walk aligns with Christ.

Emotional and physical intimacy should match the level of commitment in the friendship. Your emotional investment in a relationship with a love interest should match the level of commitment you have both demonstrated. If he is not committed to you, your emotions should not be very strong.

The world encourages dating multiple people, often simultaneously, without any responsibility to each other. Lust, sexual gratification, and selfish desires come first while spiritual maturity, character, and integrity come later. Consequently, many people are hurt because they are confused and were led to believe that a person was more committed to them than they actually were. Lives are often devastated by careless choices.

Patience is key. Set limits on how much you let a person into your emotional and physical space. There are several ways to protect them. You can control your space by controlling the frequency of communication, limiting the time you spend with a love interest in person, controlling your physical interactions, and keeping your thoughts and emotions in check.

Limit information that you initially share with someone. Do not assume that the person you are interested in has good moral character. Abusers like to use what you say to determine if you are an easy target and to find ways to manipulate you. Minimize details about past relationships and only share this information after the person has earned your trust. Information should be shared gradually over time and communication should be mutual.

Do not jump into a relationship or marriage and do not allow someone to pressure you into a relationship. It is not appropriate to spend all of your free time with or profess your undying love for a love interest two weeks after meeting him. Be on alert if he is suggesting this.

In modern times, most dating relationships encourage some kind of physical intimacy like kissing, touching, or sex. But avoiding intimate physical contact is an absolute necessity for maintaining a pure lifestyle. Be intentional about avoiding inappropriate physical interaction or activity that leads to sex. You are not to be conformed to this world but to be transformed by the renewal of your mind. You cannot live like everyone else.

Here are some guidelines to avoid sexual interaction and maintain a sexually pure lifestyle.

1. Only date a Christian who lives a sexually pure lifestyle.

2. Pace yourself appropriately in a relationship and do not move too fast. Be mindful about the information you share with others. Do not get attached to someone before you know their character.

3. Avoid places that encourage sinful behavior or sexual immorality, like nightclubs and bars.

4. Avoid lengthy and late night encounters and phone calls with the opposite sex. Late nights and lengthy phone calls create an atmosphere of intimacy where emotional bonds are likely to be established.

5. Avoid being alone with someone of the opposite sex for long periods of time. In the beginning of dating, avoid intimate environments. Arrange meetings in public

places like coffee shops or places that involve activities like bowling, parks, outdoor concerts, etc.

6. Be mindful of your clothing and ensure it is not sexually enticing.

7. Be mindful of your speech and body language to make sure you are not suggesting sexual activity.

8. Your home is your sanctuary. Do not invite someone of the opposite sex into your home, do not go to their home.

9. Don't hold hands, kiss, or engage in any other behavior that may stir up intimacy or sexual desires.

10. Do not dress in an overly seductive manner. 1 Corinthians 8:9 tells us to be careful so that we do not become a stumbling block for the weak.

11. Don't accept gifts from someone if you don't want to.

12. Don't always go along with someone else's desires or plans.

13. Don't go out of your way for someone who is not doing the same for you.

14. Don't allow someone to play games with you, lie, or cheat on you.

15. Don't allow someone to treat you like less, when you are giving the person more.

Your Boyfriend is Not Your Husband

For many years, I saw nothing wrong with being loving or giving my body to whoever I was dating so long as I liked him and he showed he cared about me. I enjoy treating others well, and I considered my generosity a defining factor of who I was. If he was nice to me, I saw nothing wrong with cooking or cleaning for him, taking trips together, meeting each other's families and many other selfless acts. I now realize that my behavior was inappropriate and I was giving far more of myself than I should have. If I was not so generous with my time and affection, I would have quickly realized that these people did not love me, but were simply looking to take advantage of me.

Your boyfriend is not your husband. You should not be performing domestic duties for someone you are only dating. You do not have to prove that you are a "good" woman or that you are a great cook. These things about you will be revealed at the right time. Dating is also not the time to impress him in the bedroom. You are not in a competition to win his affection. In the initial stages of meeting someone, don't go out of your way or abandon your other interests and commitments. Be kind and keep favors simple. For instance, unless you are in a deeply committed relationship that is definitely leading to marriage, do not cook him meals or buy him gifts. Do not assist with his responsibilities such as his children. There is a difference between sending a man you've known for two months a birthday card and buying him a luxury watch. The man you are dating should not be reaping the same benefits as if he were your husband.

Let him take the lead and let him pursue you. Your energy and effort should never be above his. It is a man's role to pursue you. A man who desires you wants to impress you, and you should expect him to want to. Just don't let his interest get the best of you. Be sober and use wisdom. Some other practical guidelines are: (1) don't be overly generous because he is buying flowers and gifts. (2) Don't accept expensive gifts before your relationship reaches a serious level. Some gifts are to encourage you to let your guard down or to manipulate you into having sex. Accepting expensive gifts also leads to resentment by the other person if you decide that you no longer want to be involved. The Holy Spirit will guide you.

Dating vs. Courting

Courting eliminates the pitfalls of becoming too emotionally invested in someone who does not have the right intentions or who is not right for you. It establishes boundaries and gives you an opportunity to observe a person's character and get to know them on a deeper level so that you can make clear decisions before your relationship takes the next step.

If God wants us to save ourselves for marriage to one person, then it is not necessary for us to be in and out of romantic relationships. Not only is romantic involvement with different people not necessary, but the revolving door of failed relationships is devastating to your self-esteem. Many people are carrying around old wounds from past failed relationships. Those wounds seriously impact the way you feel about yourself and the way you treat others. God is deeply concerned about your emotional well-being. He is also concerned for anyone you date. God knows what's best for you. You'll have a stronger relationship with God and He can use you more when you are not walking around angry, bitter, or hurt because you have been mistreated.

The Bible tells us to guard our heart, because out of it flows the issues of life. By choosing to date in a way that honors God, you protect yourself from experiencing the pain of rejection and the effects of sin. When you date with a purpose, you will only consider someone who is at least equally committed in his walk with God. Proof of his walk with God means that he studies the Word, is obedient, and demonstrates self-control in addition to all the other fruits of the Holy Spirit.

When a person you consider marrying is living a sexually pure lifestyle, you are more likely to trust in him as your spouse. Consider if you or your future spouse takes a business trip, or when you have a verbal disagreement. A spiritually mature person is more trustworthy, and less likely to act selfishly or impulsively. There are many repercussions to marrying someone who does not have control over his flesh. Sexual immorality puts a significant strain on marriages and destroys many families. A man who lacks the ability to control his flesh prior to marriage is the type of person who is prone to pornography, extra-marital affairs, or exposing you to a sexually transmitted disease. Additionally, a person who cannot control his sexual urges is dangerous and puts you at an increased risk of violent love triangles.

Mindful Dating

Watch where you go and avoid places where sexual immorality and lust flourishes. Avoiding places where lust is encouraged protects you from predators who are looking for someone to gratify their flesh. A bar or night club is not an atmosphere that is conducive to meeting someone who is serious about their walk with Christ. Men in these places are probably not thinking about your relationship with God. Often what people are attracted to in these types of places is shallow.

Do not be loyal to someone who is not loyal to you. The closer you allow someone to be to you emotionally, the more the intimacy heightens, opening the door to lust.

The Bible tells us not to defraud each other (1 Corinthians 7:5; Matthew 5:37). There is no point in becoming emotionally entangled in a relationship that leads to nowhere. This is not fair to you or the other person who might be a better candidate for someone else.

When you are doing things that align with your divine purpose, you don't have time to waste on random people. Your time and energy become much more valuable. Dating with a purpose does not mean that any person you go on a date with you will want to marry. It means that you will only date a man that is walking with Christ and has all the attributes that make him a suitable husband. As partners in marriage, you should be leading each other to Christ. Dating with a purpose eliminates unnecessary partners and makes you available for the person that God has for you. This person will not mistreat you and will be capable of being a faithfully devoted husband.

When I made these changes, my life changed dramatically. Although my dating life came to a complete halt, abusers were no longer drawn to me. I was not in environments where abusers lurk, and I was not attracted to men who I knew were not devoted to their walk with Christ or did not value me. I began to understand more about who I was in Christ and that I am valuable to God's kingdom. I am much more emotionally stable and I have more peace.

As you continue to grow in Christ, people who are not sincere will fall by the wayside. A God-fearing man who values you will be honest about his intentions. He will not mislead you into thinking that he is more into you than he really is. He will respect your boundaries and your commitment to live for Christ, since he is living for Christ. His first concern is his relationship with God. Because you are God's child, he loves you foremost as his sister in Christ. He will treat you with the utmost respect because this is what God commands us to do.

Additional Meditation Scriptures

Romans 12:9-10 NKJV: "Let love be without hypocrisy. Abhor what is evil. Cling to what is good. Be kindly affectionate to one another with brotherly love, in honor giving preference to one another."

Galatians 5:22-24 NIV: "But the fruit of the Spirit is love, joy, peace, forbearance, kindness, goodness, faithfulness, gentleness and self-control. Against such things there is no law. Those who belong to Christ Jesus have crucified the flesh with its passions and desires."

1 John 2:16 KJV: "For all that is in the world, the lust of the flesh, and the lust of the eyes, and the pride of life, is not of the Father, but is of the world."

2 Timothy 2:22 NASB: "Now flee from youthful lusts and pursue righteousness, faith, love and peace, with those who call on the Lord from a pure heart."

Proverbs 19:21 ESV: "Many are the plans in the mind of a man, but it is the purpose of the LORD that will stand."

Prayer:

Lord, help me to identify and eliminate habits that are destructive. Remind me how much You value me. Give me wisdom in dating so that I honor You. Let my lifestyle be reflective of You. Amen.

CHAPTER 12
PURSUE GOD'S PLAN

Scriptures

Romans 8:28 KJV: "And we know that all things work together for good to them that love God, to them who are the called according to his purpose."

Exodus 9:16 NIV: "But I have raised you up for this very purpose, that I might show you my power and that my name might be proclaimed in all the earth."

Philippians 2:12-13 NIV: "Therefore, my dear friends, as you have always obeyed—not only in my presence, but now much more in my absence—continue to work out your salvation with fear and trembling, for it is God who works in you to will and to act in order to fulfill his good purpose."

1 Corinthians 12:4-12 KJV: "Now there are diversities of gifts, but the same Spirit. And there are differences of administrations, but the same Lord. And there are diversities of operations, but it is the same God which worketh all in all. But the manifestation of the Spirit is given to every man to profit withal. For to one is given by the Spirit the word of wisdom; to another the word of knowledge by the same Spirit; To another faith by the same Spirit; to another the gifts of healing by the same Spirit; To another the working of miracles; to another prophecy; to another discerning of spirits; to another divers kinds of tongues; to another the interpretation of tongues: But all these worketh that one and the selfsame Spirit, dividing to every man severally as he will. For as the body is one, and hath many members, and all the members of that one body, being many, are one body: so also is Christ."

"But unto every one of us is given grace according to the measure of the gift of Christ." Ephesians 4:7 KJV. "And he gave some, apostles; and some, prophets; and some, evangelists; and some, pastors and teachers; For the perfecting of the saints, for the work of the ministry, for the edifying of the body of Christ." Ephesians 4:11-12 KJV.

Recognize Your Gifts

Now that you know you are forgiven, take steps towards pursuing God's purpose for you. God has a plan for your life. You are important even if you don't feel you have anything special to offer, even if you are not considered important by others. God created you to be unique. There is no person in the world that has what you have or can do exactly what you can.

The first step is to recognize what your gifts are and to develop them. Your gifts and experiences are key in determining your purpose. God gives us spiritual gifts to build up the body of Christ and equip God's people for service (Ephesians 4:12). Your unique set of gifts, talents, and experiences make you the only person capable of completing the task assigned to you.

Your gifts are expressions of God's grace. You did nothing to get them. 1 Corinthians 12:7-11 illustrates different kinds of gifts given to us by the Holy Spirit. Spiritual gifts include: wisdom, knowledge, faith, healing, miracles, prophecy, discernment of spirits, speaking in tongues, and the interpretation of tongues. The Bible also describes how God uses our gifts in the church through apostles, prophets, teachers, miracles, gifts of healing, helping, administration, and various kinds of tongues (1 Corinthians 12:28-31 ESV).

The Bible commands us to use these gifts. Your gifts are valuable to the kingdom. There are people assigned to you who are desperately waiting on you to achieve your purpose. You fulfilling your purpose is important because there are souls at stake that He wants to save. Your specific gifts, experiences, and passion will inspire, encourage, and motivate them.

Ask God for revelation in this area. Take a spiritual gifts assessment. As you spend time with God, He will reveal your gifts and talents to be used to advance His purpose.

Reflect on Your Experiences

When you pray, reflect on your own experiences and the things you think you are good at. While you are seeking His will, God will use certain people to reveal the truth to you. What if the people God has used to help you chose to be disobedient? You might still be lost. What if there were no preachers or teachers ministering the Word? What if they chose a life of mediocrity? What if no one knew how to pray? What if singers didn't sing or write music for God? Think about how God uses music to draw billions of people to Himself.

In addition to your gifts, what experiences do you have that have shaped you? The pain of my past and the insight that God gave me to overcome my circumstances gave me a passion to help others. Now, it is my desire to share this knowledge with others, just as He helped me.

You may also have some natural talents. Can you sing, act, or dance? Are you creative or do you have an eye for fashion? Are you a great listener? There are many things that you can do for the kingdom that are not preaching in a pulpit. All are valuable.

Develop Your Gifts

Now that you have an idea of what your gifts and talents are, begin to work on them. Developing your talents to be used by God takes work and sacrifice. For most people walking in their purpose, success is the result of tremendous sacrifice, struggle, and being discouraged, but simply never giving up. As your faith grows and as you become more mature in Christ, God may reveal more gifts to you. Just like NBA players spend many hours a day training, practicing, strengthening their bodies, and studying tapes, so should you devote yourself to developing your gifts and talents.

Never Give Up

Don't ever give up on your dreams. Success requires tremendous sacrifice and determination. There is no easy road to success, despite common misperceptions. You may not feel worthy of the assignment God has given you. Moses did not feel qualified to lead his people out of captivity. However, despite Moses's feelings, he was obedient. What would have happened had Moses chosen to ignore God's calling and not lead the children out of Egypt?

There will be people who will discourage you and you will face many obstacles. When people put you down, ignore them and work. Your trials and suffering are by God's design to build character. The Bible tells us to "glory in tribulations also: knowing that tribulation worketh patience; And patience, experience; and experience, hope." Romans 5:3-4 KJV. God will give you grace to overcome your obstacles. No one can stop what God has for you. However, you can hinder your success by not trying or giving up when it gets hard.

Fortify yourself by spending time with God. Many very successful people were initially rejected, but they never gave up despite their fears and their circumstances. Don't be discouraged because you don't have the background or resources that you think you need.

Be Bold

Be bold and take action. God has already given you the tools you need to pursue His purpose. Do things you are afraid to do. Take well-thought-out risks. The Bible says faith without works is dead. It is okay to be afraid, but don't let fear stop you. Fear does not come from God. Ask God for resources and direction. Ask God to align you with people who can help you achieve your purpose. Take one step at a time. Let God give you momentum as you take steps toward your destiny. Babies learn to sit, then crawl, then walk, then run. With each phase, the baby gains more strength to reach the next level.

Accept failure as part of the process. Failure either guides you to do better, or points you in the right direction. It is better for you to have tried and failed than to never have tried at all. Use your experiences and your knowledge to help someone else who may be struggling in the same area.

Remember God cares for you. He wants to use you so that others may experience Him through you. God wants the glory in your life. God says, "And I, if I be lifted up from the earth, will draw all men unto me." John 12:32 KJV. So in whatever you do, do it unto Him. Let your life be a reflection of Christ wherever you go. Use your passion to encourage someone else, and spread His love.

Prayer:

Lord, thank you for creating me for a purpose. Reveal to me what my gifts and talents are and how You want me to use them towards my purpose. Give me the courage to walk in my purpose and the wisdom and resources to pursue it. Amen.

CHAPTER 13
EMBRACE YOUR IDENTITY IN CHRIST

Scriptures

Psalm 139:14 KJV: "I will praise thee; for I am fearfully and wonderfully made: marvellous are thy works; and that my soul knoweth right well."

Ephesians 4:21-24 NKJV: "If indeed you have heard Him and have been taught by Him, as the truth is in Jesus: that you put off, concerning your former conduct, the old man which grows corrupt according to the deceitful lusts, and be renewed in the spirit of your mind, and that you put on the new man which was created according to God, in true righteousness and holiness."

Your Identity is in Christ

Your identity is not in your experiences or what others think of you. Your identity is in Christ. The entire Bible illustrates God's love for you. Each book in the Bible meticulously describes God's longing to be in relationship with you. Every Scripture, every psalm, every author, and ultimately Christ's death and resurrection proves God's love for you and His desire to bless you here on Earth and eternally in Heaven. God created you in His image. You are fearfully and wonderfully made. The Bible says that He formed your inward parts and knitted you together in your mother's womb (Psalm 139:13 ESV). Even the "very hairs of your head" are numbered (Matthew 10:30 KJV).

Regardless of how you came into the world, God is your heavenly Father. God did not create you randomly or by accident. You were handpicked. God chose you before the creation of the world. You did not choose Him, but He chose you. God has adopted you into His kingdom and you are a child of God, an heir (Galatians 4:7 KJV). You are "a royal priesthood"; you are holy and peculiar (1 Peter 2:9). To be holy means you are set apart, not like the rest of the world. Holy is defined as "exalted or worthy of complete devotion as one perfect in goodness and righteousness."[42] God is holy and He picked you to be a light in a world of darkness. Your shining glorifies Him. He wants you to share the gospel with others who may be trapped in darkness (1 Peter 2:9).

As a follower of Christ, you have a new identity. You are a new person, created in righteousness and holiness (Ephesians 4:24). You are not your own, but you belong to Him. You are His workmanship, created in Christ Jesus to do good works (Ephesians 2:10). As a believer, you have the power of Christ inside of you. You are a valuable member of the body of Christ, and every member works together to edify the body in love (1 Corinthians 12:14-27).

Nothing You Experience is by Happenstance

Nothing that you experienced and nothing you will go through is by happenstance. The Bible says, "we know that all things work together for good to them that love God, to them who are the called according to his purpose"

(Romans 8:28 KJV). Your value does not depend on what others think of you. It does not matter what happened to you or what people said to you. It does not matter what you did. It does not matter if your mother or your father rejected you. Your worth is not based on your family, accomplishments, social status, wealth, your education, or anything else. What matters is what God thinks of you. You have an important role and a destiny to fulfill.

Christ was rejected by those He loved, persecuted, and lied on. He was betrayed by people closest to Him. Christ came down in the form of a man to suffer and die for you. There is no pain that you can experience that He does not feel; your suffering is not in vein. Your experiences have given you compassion, wisdom, courage, and insight. God can use your pain to free someone else. This is your purpose. You must go through something to effectively help someone else. Your gifts and your experiences are the key to someone else's freedom.

God Loves You

God loves you infinitely. If you were to count His thoughts towards you, they are more than the sand (Psalm 139:18). After Adam and Eve sinned against God, we lost our relationship with our Creator, and we were forever sentenced to death. Christ died for me and for you, so that we might have a relationship with our Heavenly Father. "For God so loved the world, that he gave his only begotten Son, that whosoever believeth in him should not perish, but have everlasting life" (John 3:16 KJV). There is no higher love than God's love. John says, there is no greater love than someone that lays "down his life for his friends" (John 15:13 KJV).

God loves us so much that when we were still dead to Him because of our sins, He made us alive together with Christ. He saved us by His grace. The Bible says, He has raised you up and seated you with Him in heavenly places in Christ Jesus, so that He might show you the immeasurable riches of His grace and kindness toward you. For by grace you have been saved through faith. There is nothing that you did to deserve His grace; it is the gift of God.

His love is eternal. Nothing can separate you from His love. Paul declares: "For I am persuaded, that neither death, nor life, nor angels, nor principalities, nor powers, nor things present, nor things to come, nor height, nor depth, nor any other creature, shall be able to separate us from the love of God, which is in Christ Jesus our Lord" (Romans 8:38 KJV).

Walk in Your Purpose

Your greatest gift to God is to fulfill your purpose, which ultimately glorifies Him and edifies His kingdom. Use your gifts to serve Him and spread the love of Christ. 1 John 2:27 KJV says, "But the anointing which ye have received of him abideth in you, and ye need not that any man teach you: but as the same anointing teacheth you of all things, and is truth, and is no lie, and even as it hath taught you, ye shall abide in him." Paul and Timothy encourage believers to honor God with our gifts, to take them seriously, and to treat others with love so that Christ can be glorified. Ephesians 4:1-3 KJV says, "I therefore, the prisoner of the Lord, beseech you that ye walk worthy of the vocation wherewith ye are called, with all lowliness and meekness, with longsuffering, forbearing one another in love; endeavoring to keep the unity of the Spirit in the bond of peace."

1 Timothy 4:14 ESV instructs us to "not neglect the gift" we have, which was given to us by "prophecy when the council of elders laid their hands" on us. Jesus asks us to deny ourselves, take up our cross, and follow Him. Considering all He has done for us, it is our reasonable sacrifice. He promises that whatever we lose by following Him, He will give us far more! Jesus declares that "there is no one who has left house or brothers or sisters or mother or father or children or lands, for my sake, and for the gospel, who shall "not receive a hundredfold now in this time, houses and brothers and sisters and mothers and children and lands, with persecutions, and in the age to come eternal life" (Mark 10:29-30 ESV).

Activate Your Spiritual Weapons

As a child of God, you possess weapons to encourage yourself and to help yourself counter the attacks of the enemy. The Bible says, we don't wrestle "against flesh and blood, but against principalities, against powers, against the rulers of the darkness of this world, against spiritual wickedness in high places" (Ephesians 6:12 KJV).

You will face many obstacles and trials. You will face rejection and setbacks. You will fall down at times. Your fight is not easy, but you already have the victory in Christ Jesus (1 John 5:4). Remain steadfast in your faith. We do not wrestle with flesh and blood (Ephesians 6:12). Paul advises us to put on the whole armor of God, that we may be able to withstand the attacks from the enemy (Ephesians 6:11). Ephesians 6:14-18 KJV lists the types of armor to fortify you. First Paul instructs us to "stand therefore, having your loins girt about with truth" (Ephesians 6:14 KJV). The truth is the Word of God.[41] When you know the truth, the enemy cannot deceive you. We are also to put on "the breast-plate of righteousness" (Ephesians 6:14 KJV). God protects the righteous. The Bible says that God gives wisdom to the righteous and He is a buckler for those "that walk uprightly" (Proverbs 2:7). God will fight for you (Psalm 35:1). You can run to Him when you are persecuted and you are safe (Proverbs 18:10). Therefore, live according to God's will and always demonstrate love, kindness, and humility to others. Honor God with your attitude, behavior, and words to align with that of Christ. God is sovereign. There is no enemy that is a match for God.

"And your feet shod with the preparation of the gospel of peace" (Ephesians 6:15 KJV). Prepare for the attacks of the enemy by reading and studying the Word daily. God's Word brings peace. Through your relationship with Christ, God will give you "the peace that surpasses all understanding," which will guard your heart and mind in the midst of your storms (Philippians 4:7 NKJV). Through studying God's Word, you have peace because you know that God is with you. He is working things out in your favor.

Next, we should "take the helmet of salvation, and the sword of the Spirit" (Ephesians 6:17 NKJV). A helmet protects your head which contains your thoughts. When you are saved, God's Word will renew your mind with the Holy Spirit. The Holy Spirit is a comforter that reminds you of God's love for you (John 14:26 KJV). The Holy Spirit encourages you in moments of weakness and strengthens you so that you may resist the enemy. He brings peace and aligns your thoughts with the thoughts of Christ so that you are not easily influenced by material things, popularity, or other things that the world offers. Instead, your focus is on things that are above (Colossians 3:2).

The sword of the Spirit is the Word of God (Ephesians 6:17). The Word of God is powerful and sharp (Hebrews 4:12). It is "a discerner of the thoughts and intents of the heart" (Hebrews 4:12 KJV). Studying God's Word gives you the ability to discern good from evil, and to rightly distinguish the truth from the enemy's lies. Rather than reacting to every negative situation, insult, or tragedy with anxiety, malice, strife, anger, bitterness, or deception, you will not worry because you know that God is for you!

We should "above all, take on the shield of faith, to quench all the fiery darts of the wicked (Ephesians 6:16 KJV). The Bible says that "faith is the substance of things hoped for, the evidence of things not seen" (Hebrews 11:1

KJV). Having faith in Christ is the most important weapon since it is your faith that compels you to do things His way, even when it doesn't make sense based on your present circumstances. God moves through your faith. By His grace, it is your faith that saves you and compels you to study God's Word and develop a relationship with Him. God works in the supernatural, not the natural. His thoughts are above our thoughts and His ways are above our ways (Isaiah 55:8-9 KJV). Your faith glorifies God and allows Him to order your steps to bless you and present opportunities to achieve victories that would have been impossible for you to achieve without Him. It is your faith that pleases God (Hebrews 11:6: KJV).

Therefore, let God have full reign over your life. You will face uncertainties and there will be times you are afraid; however, God is a man who cannot lie (Titus 1:2 KJV). Be bold and courageous! Get outside of your comfort zone and trust God over your circumstances. See what God does in your life. God knows the evil plots and tactics of the enemy and He wants you to win. Your words have power. Throw the word back at the devil when he tries to attack you. Speak it out loud. You are a warrior for Christ. You are not a victim. You are more than a conqueror (Romans 8:37 KJV)!

Finally, Paul says to pray always with supplication in the Spirit, and watch with all perseverance and supplication for all saints (Ephesians 6:18). Praying is vital to strengthen your relationship with God. Prayer is how we communicate with God. God likes to commune with you. Sometimes we don't know what to pray for, but the Holy Spirit will make intercession for us (Romans 8:26). Because we have been justified through Christ's death, we are able to access God directly. Pray often. Pray for yourself and others. God answers prayers. Your prayers don't have to be long to be effective. And remember to always thank God when you pray.

Take Care of Your Body

Your body is a temple of the Holy Spirit. God has entrusted you with your body, but it does not belong to you (1 Corinthians 6:19). Strive for good health. Eat a healthy diet. What you put into your body has an effect on you. Changing my diet dramatically improved my mood, the way I looked, my skin, and how I felt about myself. You're worth it.

Implement regular physical activity. Go for a walk, ride a bike, sweat it out at the gym, do yoga, or take a workout class. Do something you enjoy that gets your heart pumping. Physical activity helps you manage your stress levels, improves your self-esteem, and is good for your health.

Get proper rest. Rest is how your body rejuvenates itself. Getting proper rest can be tough when you have many responsibilities. However, this is a spiritual fight. To walk in your purpose effectively, you must be physically, mentally, and emotionally prepared to fight. It is easier for the enemy to control your thoughts and manipulate your body when you don't get enough sleep. Your health is important. Challenge yourself to become the best person you can be, inside and outside.

Minimize Distractions

Another way the enemy attempts to control us is with distractions. Recognize areas in your life that are distractions. Pursuing your purpose means that you have to prioritize your time. Ensure that you are spending time on things that are fruitful, like steps toward your purpose, developing your gifts, developing godly relationships, and spending time with God. Minimize your time on things that are not fruitful, like social media, internet shopping, or entertaining people who do not serve you. No day is promised to you. Your time is valuable.

Even though your time is limited, make time to do something special for yourself. Women tend to be nurturers by nature. Sometimes we find ourselves constantly taking care of others while neglecting ourselves. Don't neglect yourself for others. It is okay for you to enjoy life! Do something that you enjoy from time to time. Have some quiet time to yourself. Enjoy a relaxing bath. Go on a trip. Explore a new hobby. You are a much better servant when you are good to yourself.

Exercise Your Faith

Have faith in God. As your faith grows, so does your ability to take bold steps towards becoming the person He created you to be. While we are not saved by works, God will bless you for choosing to be obedient to Him. As He continues to bless you, your faith will grow. Eventually, you will become so firm in His Word that you have immovable, unshakeable faith. God uses your faith to do mighty things through you to glorify Him. It is our faith, not our good works, which pleases God. Without faith it is impossible to please God. Therefore, take bold steps and put your faith in God.

Now that you know that your identity is in Christ, abide in Him. Trust God, not your circumstances, and not man. Psalm 118:8 declares that it is better for us to put our trust in the Lord than to put confidence in man. While God uses people to help us, people can be a hindrance. Do not trust man over God. Be wise. Listen to advice from people who care about you and who you can trust. Don't ignore your own judgment and know that God's Word always prevails over the opinions of others. Remember people are flawed. People will sometimes judge you based on what they perceive. Man can't see in you what God sees. Only God knows all your experiences. Doing things to please people is not what God wants. Ephesians 6:6-7 KJV tells us to serve God, "Not with eyeservice, as menpleasers; but as the servants of Christ, doing the will of God from the heart; with good will doing service, as to the Lord, and not to men."

Ultimately, it is God, not man, who takes care of you. You must meditate on the Word of God to know who to listen to, and who not to listen to. Remember, God will never leave you or forsake you (Deuteronomy 31:6 KJV). Therefore, put your faith in God. Watch what He does in your life. You have the power to break free!

Yolanda R. Cumbess, JD

Additional Meditation Scriptures

Genesis 1:27 KJV: "So God created man in his own image, in the image of God created he him; male and female created he them."

Jeremiah 1:5 KJV: "Before I formed thee in the belly I knew thee; and before thou camest forth out of the womb I sanctified thee, and I ordained thee a prophet unto the nations."

Ephesians 4:24 KJV: "And that ye put on the new man, which after God is created in righteousness and true holiness."

Ephesians 1:4-5 KJV: "According as he hath chosen us in him before the foundation of the world, that we should be holy and without blame before him in love: Having predestinated us unto the adoption of children by Jesus Christ to himself, according to the good pleasure of his will."

Ephesians 2:10 KJV: "For we are his workmanship, created in Christ Jesus unto good works, which God hath before ordained that we should walk in them."

1 Peter 2:9 KJV: "But ye are a chosen generation, a royal priesthood, an holy nation, a peculiar people; that ye should show forth the praises of him who hath called you out of darkness into his marvellous light."

Romans 8:17 KJV: "And if children, then heirs; heirs of God, and joint-heirs with Christ; if so be that we suffer with him, that we may be also glorified together."

Romans 8:29-30 NIV: "For those God foreknew he also predestined to be conformed to the image of his Son, that he might be the firstborn among many brothers and sisters. And those he predestined, he also called; those he called, he also justified; those he justified, he also glorified."

Prayer:

Lord, thank you for your unending love for me. Thank you for choosing me. I acknowledge You as my Lord and Savior. Thank you for sacrificing Your life so that I may have life. Thank you for giving me an identity in You. I'm surrendering my life to You so that You may be glorified through me. Amen.

REFERENCES

Chapter 1: What is a Destructive Relationship?

1. Abuse defined: Is This Abuse? loveisrespect.org, Loveisrespect, ©2017, https://www.loveisrespect.org/is-this-abuse/.

2. Sutherland Shooting: CBS News, Texas Church Shooting in Sutherland Springs: Latest on Investigation, Copyright © 2018 CBS Interactive Inc., www.cbsnews.com, https://www.cbsnews.com/live-news/texas-church-shooting-sutherland-springs-devin-patrick-kelley-live-updates/.

3. Abuse statistics: Olga Khazan, Health: Nearly Half of All Murdered Women Are Killed by Romantic Partners, A new CDC report suggests that domestic violence is a major cause of death for women, www.theatlantic.com, TheAtlantic.com Copyright (c) 2018 by The Atlantic Monthly Group, July, 20, 2017, https://www.theatlantic.com/health/archive/2017/07/homicides-women/534306/.

4. Abuse Statistics: Alanna Vaglanos, Women: 30 Shocking Domestic Violence Statistics That Remind Us It's An Epidemic, Statistic from World Health Organization, huffingtonpost.com, ©2018 Oath Inc, HuffPost MultiCultural/HPMG News, 10/23/2014, Updated Dec 06, 2017, https://www.huffingtonpost.com/2014/10/23/domestic-violence-statistics_n_5959776.html.

5. Red Flags: Steve McCormick, The Flags Of NASCAR, Thought.co, Dotdash Publishing, March 18, 2017, https://www.thoughtco.com/flags-of-nascar-2471877.

6. Red Flags: Abigail Brenner, M.D., 10 Relationship Red Flags; Ignore them at your own risk, www.psychology-today.com, Psychology Today © 2018 Sussex Publishers, LLC, July 29, 2014, https://www.psychologytoday.com/us/blog/in-flux/201407/10-relationship-red-flags.

7. Red Flags: Red Flags of Abuse, www.nnedv.org, NNEDV, National Network to End Domestic Violence, © 2017. https://nnedv.org/content/red-flags-of-abuse/.

8. Physical Abuse: What are the different types of dating abuse, www.loveisrespect.org, LoveisRespect.org, ©2017, https://www.loveisrespect.org/is-this-abuse/types-of-abuse/.

9. Sexual Abuse: Sexual Abuse, www.apa.org, Article adapted from Encyclopedia of Psychology, American Psychological Association, © 2018 American Psychological Association, http://www.apa.org/topics/sexual-abuse/.

10. Sexual Abuse: Intimate Partner Sexual Violence, www.rainn.org, RAINN, RAINN © 2018, https://www.rainn.org/articles/intimate-partner-sexual-violence.

11. Emotional Abuse: Natasha Tracy, Emotional Abuse: Definitions, Signs, Symptoms, Examples, www.healthyplace.com, Healthy Place For Your Mental

Health, © 2018, https://www.healthyplace.com/abuse/emotional-psychological-abuse/psychological-abuse-definition-signs-and-symptoms.

12. Antisocial Personality Disorder: Steve Bressert, Ph.D., Antisocial Personality Disorder Symptoms, psychcentral.com, PsychCentral, ©1995-2018, https://psychcentral.com/disorders/antisocial-personality-disorder/symptoms/.

13. Antisocial Personality Disorder: Overview, Antisocial Personality Disorder, wwwmayoclinic.org, © 1998-2018 Mayo Foundation for Medical Education and Resources (MFMER), https://www.mayoclinic.org/diseases-conditions/antisocial-personality-disorder/symptoms-causes/syc-20353928.

14. Sociopath: Tarra Bates-Duford, Ph.D., MFT, Relationship Corner, Psychopath vs Sociopath: 16 Key Differences; www.psychcentral.com; Copyright © 1995-2018 Psych Central; https://blogs.psychcentral.com/relationship-corner/2018/08/psychopath-vs-sociopath-16-key-differences/.

15. Sociopath: Kara Mayer Robinson, www.webmd.com, WebMD LLC © 1995-2018, https://www.webmd.com/mental-health/features/sociopath-psychopath-difference#1.

16. Psychopath: Charles Montaldo, Characteristics of the Pyschopathic Personality, Recognizing Psychopathic

Traits and Behavior, www.thought.com, Thought.Co, DotDash Publishing, December 14, 2017, https://www. thoughtco.com/characteristics-of-the-psychopath-ic-personality-973128.

17. Psychopath: Fiona Guy - Psychology of a Murder, The Mind of a Psychopath: The Psychopathic Killer, www.crimetraveller.com, Crime Traveller Online Resources, © 2018 Crime Traveller, https://www. crimetraveller.org/2015/07/inside-mind-of-psychopath-psychopathic-killer/.

18. Narcissistic Personality Disorder: Overview: Narcissitic Personality Disorder, www.mayoclinic.org, © 1998-2018 Mayo Foundation for Medical Education and Resources (MFMER), https://www.mayoclinic.org/diseases-conditions/narcissistic-personality-disorder/symptoms-causes/syc-20366662.

19. The "Victim": Darlene Lancer, J.D., M.F.T., Symptoms of Codependency, www.psychcentral.com , https://psych-central.com/lib/symptoms-of-codependency/.

20. Codependent Relationships: Beth Gilbert, Do You Have Codependent Personality?, www.everydayhealth.com, Everyday Health, Ziff Davis LLC., © 1996-2018 https://www.everydayhealth.com/emotional-health/do-you-have-a-codependent-personality.aspx.

21. Drug Abuse: Eric Patterson, MSCP, NCC, LPC, How Drug Addiction Hurts Relationships, www.drugabuse.

com, DrugAbuse.Com- operated by Recovery Brands LLC., subsidiary of American Addiction Centers, © DrugAbuse.com 2018. https://drugabuse.com/library/addiction-hurts-relationships/.

22. The "Criminal": Elinor Greenberg, PhD; How to Avoid Toxic Relationships, July 8, 2018; How To Avoid Toxic Relationships; www.pyschologytoday.com; Psychology Today © 2018 Sussex Publishers, LLC; https://www.psychologytoday.com/us/blog/understanding-narcissism/2007/how-avoid-toxic-relationships.

23. Emergency Contact Info: National Coalition Against Domestic Violence, NCADV, Get Help, www.ncadv.org, NCADV, National Domestic Violence Hotline: 1-800-799-SAFE (7233) or TTY 1-800-787-3224; hotline. womenslaw.org.

Chapter 2: Authentic Love

1. Respect defined: Merriam Webster Dictionary, Respect:www.merriamwebster.com, © 2018 Merriam-Webster, Incorporated, https://www.merriam-webster.com/dictionary/respect

2. Characteristics of Healthy Relationships: The Equality Wheel Explained: What is it and how is it different from the Power and Control Wheel?, By domesticshelters.org, © 2018 Theresa's Fund, Inc., https://www.

domesticshelters.org/domestic-violence-articles-infor-mation/the-equality-wheel-explained, August 24, 2015.

Chapter 3: Recognize Destructive Patterns

1. Stronghold Defined: Stronghold, Merriam-Webster, www.merriam-webster.com, © 2018 Merriam-Webster, Incorporated, updated August 27, 2018, https://www.merriam-webster.com/dictionary/stronghold.

2. Stronghold: Evangelist Bernard Clifford, Overcoming mental strongholds & renewing your mind, www.triumphinchrist.org, http://www.triumphinchrist.org/sermons/overcoming-mental-strongholds-renewing-your-mind/.

3. Stronghold: Strongholds, www.greatbiblestudy.com, Copyrighted © 2003-2008 Robert L., http://www.greatbiblestudy.com/strongholds.php.

4. Codependent Relationship defined: Co-dependency: What Are The Signs & How To Overcome It, Feb 9, 2018, Positive Psychology Program B.V., https://positive psychologyprogram.com,https://positivepsychology program.com/co-dependency-definition-signs-work-sheets/.

5. Co-dependent Relationships Defined: Co-Dependency, www.mentalhealthamerica.net, © Copyright 2018 | Mental Health America | Formerly known as the National

Mental Health Association, downloaded 8/31/2018, http://www.mentalhealthamerica.net./co-dependency.

Chapter 4: Why Abuse Happens

1. Codependent Relationships: Linda Esposito, LCSW, September 19, 2016, 6 Signs of a Co-dependent Relationship:, www.psychologytoday.com, Psychology Today © 2018 Sussex Publishers, LLC, https://www. psychologytoday.com/us/blog/anxiety-zen/201609/6-s igns-co-dependent-relationship.

2. Codependency Symptoms: Beth Gilbert, Do You Have a Codependent Personality?, www.everydayhealth.com, https://www.everydayhealth.com/emotional-health/ do-you-have-a-co-dependent-personality.aspx.

3. Boundaries: When to Say Yes, How to Say No to Take Control of Your Life: Dr. Henry Cloud, Dr. John Townsend; Chp. 1 "A Day in a Boundaryless Life," Page 34, Published October 20th 1992 by Zondervan.

Chapter 6: Establish Healthy Boundaries

1. Boundaries: Darlene Lancer, JD, MFT, What Are Personal Boundaries? How Do I Get Some?, www.psy-chcentral.com, Copyright © 1995-2018 Psych Central, https://psychcentral.com/lib/what-are-personal-boundaries-how-do-i-get-some/.

2. Assertiveness: Assertiveness- The Importance of Being Assertive, K. A. Fareed (Fareed Siddiqui), experts-column.com, Copyright EXPERTSCOLUMN.COM © 2018, updated July 29, 2016, http://selfimprovement tips.expertscolumn.com/article/assertiveness-importance-being-assertive.

3. Types of Boundaries: M. Beard, Boundaries: Definition and Types of Boundaries, www.cross-roadsindy.com, © CrossRoads 1985-2018, http://crossroadsindy.com/counseling-and-mental-health-articles/couples-and-marriage/boundaries-definition-and-types-of-boundaries.

4. Interpersonal Boundaries: What Is An Interpersonal Boundary, www.usdrugrehabcenters.com, US Drug Rehab Centers, http://www.usdrugrehabcenters.com/the-relapse-prevention-plan/chapter-eight/what-is-an-interpersonal-boundary/.

5. Interpersonal Relationships: Leadership Qualities: Conflict Management, www.bible.org, Bible.org. 2018, https://bible.org/seriespage/19-conflict-management.

Chapter 7: Avoid Sexual Immorality

1. Sexual Immorality: True Spirituality: A Study in 1 Corinthians: 10. The Relationship Between Spirituality and Sexual Morality (1 Cor. 6:12-20), www.bible.org, © 2018 Bible.org, https://bible.org/seriespage/10-

relationship-between-spirituality-and-sexual-morali-ty-1-cor-612-20.

2. Attachments Formed: Hallie Gould, This Is What Happens to Your Brain When You Have Sex, www.theth-irty.bydie.com, © 2018 Clique Brands Inc., April 3, 2018, https://thethirty.byrdie.com/what-happens-during-sex/slide2.

Chapter 13: Embrace Your Identity in Christ

1. Spiritual Weapons: What is the full armor of God?, https://www.gotquestions.org/full-armor-of-God.html.

2. Holy Defined: Merriam-Webster, www.merriam-web-ster.com, © 2019 Merriam-Webster, Incorporated, https://www.merriam-webster.com/dictionary/holy.

Recommended Resources

1. Choosing God's Best: Wisdom for Lifelong Romance - Don Raunikar (1998). Choosing God's Best: Wisdom for Lifelong Romance. Random House. ISBN 0307568652.

2. Boundaries: When to Say Yes, How to Say No to Take Control of Your Life: Dr. Henry Cloud, Dr. John Townsend, Published October 20th 1992 by Zondervan.

3. Darlene Lancer, JD, MFT, July 17, 2018; Power, Control & Codependency, www.psychcentral.com, Copyright © 1995-2018 Psych Central, https://psychcentral.com/lib/power-control-codependency/.

4. Anointing Fall on Me: Accessing the Power of the Holy Spirit: T.D. Jakes, Copyright ©1997, Destiny Image Publishers, Inc.

Bible Sources

1. Unless otherwise indicated, scripture quotations are from the Holy Bible, King James Version. All rights reserved.

2. Scriptures marked ESV are taken from English Standard Version®. Copyright © 2001 by Crossway, a publishing ministry of Good News Publishers. All rights reserved.

3. Scriptures marked NASB are taken from the New American Standard Bible®. Copyright © 1960, 1962,

4.

5.

6.

ACKNOWLEDGMENTS

I'd like to thank the following people who encouraged me and inspired me to never give up and to go after my dreams:

Dr. Pamela Love-Manning; Dr. Tony Draper and the Finisher's Network; Daryl Dudley, CEO of Dudley's B Sharp Music Academy and She's My Daughter; Sherry Donahue-Brown M. Ed; Elder Tiffany A. Harrison; Elder Cassandra Bering; Elder Anerita Pollard; Elder Monique Garcia; Karen Woodward-Banks; and the Purposely Created Publishing Group.

ABOUT THE AUTHOR

Yolanda Cumbess was born in Houston, Texas. She earned a BS in Industrial Engineering from Texas Tech and a Juris Doctor from Loyola University New Orleans School of Law. Yolanda is now a licensed attorney, a member of the State Bar of Georgia and The District of Columbia Bar, and works as a Primary Patent Examiner at the United States Patent and Trademark Office in Alexandria, Virginia.

Yolanda obtained a ministry license in 2017 through the Higher Ground Always Abounding Assembly, Inc. Serving in various church ministries and community outreach services, she is passionate about motivating others and ministering to the needs of women and children who have been marginalized and abused. Yolanda is also the founder of Break Free Ministries and YRC Aspire Enterprises. In 2015, Yolanda was published as a contributing author of *Life Happens But You Can Finish, The Trials, Triumphs, and Truths of 12 Amazing Finishers.*

To learn more, visit her website at
www.yrcaspire.com